DATE DUE

DEC 1 3 1995	
MAY 2 0 1996	

GAYLORD   PRINTED IN U.S.A.

NASW REPRINTS

Preventive Intervention in Social Work

CAROL H. MEYER, editor

National Association of Social Workers, Inc.

1425 H Street, N.W.

Washington, D.C. 20005

Preventive Intervention in Social Work

CAROL H. MEYER, editor

National Association of Social Workers, Inc.

1425 H Street, N.W.

Washington, D.C. 20005

The articles in this collection were selected from *Social Work,* the journal
of the National Association of Social Workers, volumes 1 through 18.   They
were selected by the editor with a special view toward their flexible use in one or
another combination by students and faculty.   The articles may be
purchased either individually or as a total package of eleven articles and
Dr. Meyer's introduction.

CONTENTS

002.   Introduction / Preventive Intervention: A Goal in
        Search of a Method
        CAROL H. MEYER

003.   The Concept of Prevention in Social Work
        LYDIA RAPOPORT

004.   Social Treatment: A New-Old Helping Method
        MAX SIPORIN

005.   The Life-Space Interview
        DAVID WINEMAN

006.   New Dimensions in Reaching-out Casework
        ROBERT SUNLEY

007.   New Professional Work Roles and Their Integration
        into a Social Agency Structure
        GERALD M. SHATTUCK AND JOHN M. MARTIN

008.   Crisis Intervention: Theory in Search of a Program
        RICHARD A. PASEWARK AND DALE A. ALBERS

009.   Working with Families in Crisis: An Exploration
        in Preventive Intervention
        LYDIA RAPOPORT

010.   Crisis Intervention with Victims of Rape
        SANDRA SUTHERLAND FOX AND DONALD J. SCHERL, MD

011.   Use of Crisis Intervention in Casework with the
        Cancer Patient and His Family
        JEANNETTE R. OPPENHEIMER

012.   Crisis Intervention in an Earthquake
        HERBERT BLAUFARB AND JULES LEVINE

013.   Integrating the New Immigrant: A Model for
        Social Work Practice in Transitional States
        NAOMI GOLAN AND RUTH GRUSCHKA

Introduction / Preventive Intervention: A Goal in Search of a Method

SOCIAL WORKERS share a common dilemma with all other professional practitioners in the human services. On one hand, they seek solutions to problems and are eager to track down precise linkages between psychosocial etiology and specific treatment techniques that will effectively cure problems of people in their environments. On the other hand, they have a professional commitment to find ways to prevent those problems from occurring, at least to the extent that they have knowledge and skills to do so. Why should this be a dilemma? What prevents a professional practitioner from doing what has to be done for the whole range of social problems, whether before or after the breakdown occurs? Can it be assumed that the typical social worker is prepared to apply his knowledge and skills anywhere along the continuum from prevention to cure?

For more than two decades the profession has assumed that by putting social workers in nonclinical settings and by following the public health model of primary, secondary, and tertiary prevention, social workers could address psychosocial conditions before serious breakdown occurred. Yet the idea of prevention seems to remain just that—an idea or an abstraction, appropriate to social policy and planning perhaps, but with no clinical ring to it. Generally the question of preventive intervention has been a casework issue; for the most part group work and community organization models do not rely on therapeutic assumptions. Perhaps the current trend of bringing together all these methodologies into a single model of practice will contribute to a better resolution of the "dilemma."[1]

VALUES AND KNOWLEDGE

Until now, the mainstream of professional practice has been governed by constrictions of *values* and *knowledge,* which have served to separate preventive from therapeutic activities and thus have perpetuated the dilemma. The problem of values, of course, derives from the familiar cause-function issue discussed by Lee.[2] Lee was concerned with the increasing preoccupation in his day with techniques and method and cautioned about maintaining a commitment to "cause through social reform." The cause-function issue remains an unfortunate and historically powerful con-

Carol H. Meyer, DSW, is Professor of Social Work, Columbia University School of Social Work, New York, New York.

[1] *See,* for example, Howard Goldstein, *Social Work Practice: A Unitary Approach* (Columbia: University of South Carolina Press, 1973); and Allen Pincus and Anne Minahan, *Social Work Practice: Model and Method* (Itasca, Ill.: F. E. Peacock Publishers, 1973).

[2] Porter R. Lee, "Social Work: Cause and Function," *Proceedings of the National Conference of Social Work—San Francisco, 1929* (Chicago: University of Chicago Press, 1930).

CAO-002-C

flict over values in the field. To a large extent, those who were once called caseworkers and are presently called "clinical social workers" or "specialists in work with individuals and families" or "graduates" of concentrations in specific problem or methodological areas are still trained to treat problems that can be defined in clinical-normative terms and not necessarily to work with people who do not as yet exhibit such problems. The concept of clinical-normative refers to the idea that the primary goal of treatment is to help people achieve a higher level of psychosexual maturity. This is opposed to the idea that people are better helped through ego adaptation on whatever level of maturity they have already achieved. Since the bulk of social work services lies in the tertiary stage of prevention, it is evident that the focus of practice is defined by those who are already clients or patients.

The model of practice itself contains the seeds of the dilemma. That is, to ask the typical practitioner to apply knowledge and skills in prevention might require him to be a different type of practitioner. This is hard to do, and the request itself would exacerbate the tensions in the field. Yet how can social work assume appropriate reponsibility for prevention if its major tools are concerned with breakdown? It is important to recall that we are talking about direct practice with people to prevent psychosocial breakdown—not about social reform, legislation, or the organization of constituencies to bring about social change. The problem is more difficult when the analysis is confined to direct work with people who are in trouble, but whose trouble is not yet clinically definable. Probably, the practitioner can resolve his conflict in values through increased knowledge and skills of adaptational intervention that would serve his work in the area of prevention. It is not enough to say, "I believe." One must be able to say, "I know how."

The hallmark of professional practice is methodology. A methodology derives from a professional-philosophical framework for practice that defines its purposes, its sanctions, and its boundaries. Added to this are theories about people and their environments (in the case of social work) and the knowledge that underlies those theories. Theories are borrowed from other disciplines, evolved from practice wisdom, experimented with, or dreamed up—constructed from the armchair. Perhaps they are tested for validity against criteria of effectiveness. Sometimes the use of a particular method may be valid in one profession and invalid in another because of the differences in professional purpose, sanction, or boundaries. Thus although methodology is the key to professional accountability, it does not stand without reference to the professional-philosophical framework that governs it.

SEARCH FOR METHODOLOGY

The search for methodology in prevention has meant that social workers have had to seek a new conceptualization for practice. It is logical to think that a physician trained to recognize and treat symptoms of lead poisoning, for instance, would be competent to do so; but he would not be able to use his skills to deal with the complexities of life faced by a family living in a slum tenement painted with lead-based paint. In effect, he would be trained to detect clinical manifestations of the problem but not to prevent them. He might know the source of his patient's problem and even be motivated through a home visit to do something about it. Yet he would not be trained to cope with an unresponsive landlord, the family's fear about moving to another neighborhood, and other nonclinically defined problems he might discover during his visit. Unless he were unusual, he would return to his clinic to care for the children suffering the effects of lead poisoning.

Could one translate this example to problems faced by clients of social workers, such as neglected children, the aging, parolees returning to the community, discharged mental patients, working mothers, or foster children? In these cases it is theoretically possible to turn each person into a clinically defined problem. However, available knowledge about the systemic complexities of each would direct us to broader parameters of assessment and intervention. For example, because there are no clinical parameters for the relationship of poverty to child abuse or community attitudes toward ex-prisoners, the clinically oriented social worker (like the physician in the lead poisoning clinic) would have to ignore those situational factors that do not fit his clinical perspective. In this way the model of practice forces the social worker to avoid person-in-situation interventions and induces him to wait until opportunities for social supports are lost and the client indeed has a clinical problem. Then, ironically, the practitioner can get to work.

It is assumed here that all social work cases fit the professional definition of purpose as enhancing social functioning. When social workers are trained to view their work in this perspective, they will be able to approach people in trouble whenever they are brought to the workers' attention. Perhaps the dilemma of prevention-versus-treatment is of our own making; perhaps there is no continuum from prevention to cure. Does social work (as does medicine) really have conceptual differences between preventive intervention and therapeutic techniques? Are these differences the correct variables to distinguish practice approaches? Do they tend to exclude some people from necessary services? Social workers are debating these ideas today; some question whether the diagnosis of

psychological pathology is being used as a means test for service. There are other grounds for discussion as well, which have to do with the knowledge and theories about how people grow and develop in transaction with their environments. This direction of thinking allows the social worker to develop a methodology for preventive intervention into people's unique environments. It is separate from the concern with clinical determinants of behavior, which seems to contraindicate the development of such a practice model because it relies so heavily on purely psychological parameters.

STAGES OF PREVENTIVE INTERVENTION

What is preventive intervention? Its use in social work seems to have been derived from public health, much as the idea of psychotherapy was taken from the disease-cure model of medicine. In public health the continuum of activities is called "primary prevention," "secondary prevention," and "tertiary prevention." These activities are often classified as "health promotion and specific protection," "early diagnosis and treatment (including case-finding)," and "disability limitation and rehabilitation."

Even though the stages of intervention in public health and social work are not comparable, primary prevention in social welfare is possible through the provision of such services as income maintenance, health and mental health care, and adequate housing and day care, which are accepted as being basic to the survival of people in an urban industrialized society. Although some social work functions of planning and practice flow from primary prevention, this approach contains a built-in ambiguity about social work roles; this is especially true when the program itself (housing, for example) and not the service (social work in housing) is essential for meeting people's needs.

At the other end of the continuum, tertiary prevention is most often used by social workers in clinics, agencies, and other institutions whose clients have problems that are easily classified. Social work has a well-established practice based on experience with diagnosis of problems brought to agencies and case services that are clearly therapeutic and directed toward rehabilitation. It is familiar territory.

But when preventive intervention is discussed, it refers most often to the secondary level. Methodology is weakest at this level, even though the questions discussed are perhaps the most interesting. Would locating workers in new sites, such as well-baby clinics, social security offices, places of work, and day care centers, help identify populations-at-risk? Are there ways to recognize the potential strain or imbalance between the individual and his environment? How does one understand and work with case phenomena-in-the-making when one is trained to deal primarily with outcomes? Coping with the answers to these questions will introduce new conceptualizations of practice.

Not only is preventive intervention an uncertain field, it has its value conflicts as well. Some social workers would insist that because a person has the right to refuse help, he would have to feel motivated before he is identified as a client. Others would argue that the first obligation of social work is to offer help, and if the client participates in defining the problem and tasks to be accomplished, his self-determination is protected. But perhaps what is really new is the idea that help is not the same as treatment, that the joint decision of the worker and client to allocate tasks to improve a situation is not the same as the worker's professional diagnostic judgment about what is best in a case. Preventive intervention, as this collection of articles will indicate, is not less than or earlier or more of something. It is a different activity that derives from a new perspective.

THE ARTICLES

The articles in this collection deal with the implications for practice of preventive intervention and highlight new forms of direct work with clients. They reflect the state of the art during the long period when leading social work theoreticians began to develop models of preventive intervention. Some translated into social work methodology the only model that was available—the public health model and its derivative, crisis intervention. Others developed new models having to do with the social situation and the client's life-space or worked on new theories of practice roles and skills. When one views these articles as a whole, one can see two common characteristics: the expansion of the unit of attention or the focus of help to include environmental or situational supports and the recognition of multiple causes of problems when individuals and their environments are viewed as systemically connected. When social cases are viewed in this perspective, practitioners are immediately directed by their broader comprehension of problems to develop methodology that will serve the case appropriately.

Once the practitioner enters the client's "field" entirely, he must use new knowledge about the relationship of people to social structures, the nature of social organizations, the adaptive mechanisms individuals use to change themselves and their surroundings to maintain a psychosocial balance, and the kinds of practice roles necessary to be effective. This new knowledge is more complex than the traditional clinical ideas once used to explain the person as a mere psychological entity. What is preventive about the thrust of this new knowledge? The lack of reliance on clinical measures to "make the case," and thus the opportunity for the practitioner to provide service at any stage—early, late, simple, complex—in the progress of a problem. The conceptualization and the methodology described in the articles that follow suggest the new directions in which practitioners have moved.

Rapoport's article "The Concept of Prevention in Social Work" defines prevention as a way to *keep something from happening*. If social workers view practice in this way, they do not think in terms of tracking down causative agents. Instead they try to understand the interrelated psychological and social parts of the client's life situation so they can devise ways of intervening to alter those factors contributing to increased stress or pathology. This perspective suggests that efforts to right the imbalance between the client and his immediate environment should replace the search for specific etiology and cure. Growth and development and the ways people adapt to their environments would themselves be the model for practice.

Rapoport, ahead of her time, proposes several types of activities or "specific protection" tasks that would promote health. Taking a developmental view of social work, she sees the practitioner as a consultant to programs in agencies, hospitals, and other social institutions to which people are connected in the urban world. For example, she thinks populations-at-risk would benefit from family life education and service agencies should construct programs to enable people to cope better with their normal life tasks. Rapoport defines the concept, deals with the professional debates on prevention, and thrusts social workers directly into the primary prevention field—a field that some have considered ambiguous and outside the realm of the direct practitioner.

Preventive intervention requires greater attention to the "situation" as the milieu for the client's growth—not a usual approach for social workers. Siporin, in his article "Social Treatment: A New-Old Helping Method," comments on the continuing importance of the therapeutic objectives of personality growth and change. However, he clarifies how these objectives are inextricably entwined with structures in the social environment, particularly situations involving the family and community. To address maladaptive transactional processes between the person and situation, the array of interventive tasks would have to be wide and varied. "To keep something from happening" effectively pushes the social worker toward interventions in which, as Rapoport says, we can no longer seek specific etiology as cause and thus we can claim no specific linear relationship to ultimate outcome. If case situations are viewed as unique expressions of interlocking, reverberating, systemic phenomena, the traditional assurance that a specific cause leads to a specific effect becomes obsolete. Once in the realm of preventive intervention—especially the various situational influences on the client—the practitioner discovers that some phenomena describe unexpected developments in the client's life-style, behavior, relationships, and feelings. Thus the field of intervention is as wide open as the specific case allows. Preventive intervention might then come to mean this: When people are viewed as interacting with their social milieu, there are opportunities to right the psychosocial imbalance that are not necessarily definable in clinical terms; in fact they may prevent clinically defined pathology.

LIFE-SPACE INTERVIEW

Wineman's article "The Life-Space Interview" addresses "the clinical exploitation of life's events" in its description of practice that draws on the client's current life and uses immediate and real-life experiences both therapeutically and diagnostically. The author makes clear that the form of intervention derives from the perspective of the case and demonstrates that the life-space interview is indeed different from the traditional therapeutic interview. The life-space interview differs in these respects: its content changes because it draws on here-and-now events, its time and spatial dimensions are altered by the immediacy of the life-space, the social distance between practitioner and client diminishes and their relationship becomes closer because the practitioner becomes part of the client's life-space, and the formality of the role structure is defined in another way. This model of practice is considered to be emotional "first aid" and is thus preventive in its substance and aim. Whether it is of sufficient help in a case depends on such factors as the extent of the damage, the reverberations or spillover of the help itself, the press of the caseload, the availability of services, other resources in the client's situation, and so on. Once again, the linkages among psychosocial influences and the utility of intervening at a vulnerable point are important. Life-space as the unit of attention, like the situational approach and the programs described in specific protection, offers a new arena for social workers.

Sunley, in his article "New Dimensions in Reaching-Out Casework," uses a non-problem approach—situational casework—and cognitive casework to illustrate his expanded framework for intervention. Because this approach is addressed to unmotivated clients who do not define their difficulties as problems, social workers would have to be located in or at least have influence on institutions and allied services where clients go for other reasons. The enterprising practitioner might recognize opportunities for early prevention and use of indirect intervention methods to ease the way for people who are not, strictly speaking, in the role of client. Thus situational casework is similar to the life-space concept in that it emphasizes the value of having the social worker present in the client's life, rather than just reviewing the client's report of how it was. This sharing of a situation affects the traditional allocation of tasks between clients and social worker and changes the typical therapeutic relationship and content of the work they do together.

Cognitive casework is seen as a new facet in ego-strengthening and is directed toward lessening the cognitive deficiencies of socially deprived people. It introduces social workers to a broad arena for activity in developing ego functioning. Social workers are only beginning to understand the therapeutic effects of enlarging the individual's cognitive world and enriching his capacity to enjoy cultural and intellectual pursuits. They are on the brink of discovering that self-image, for example, might be enhanced through a person's improved sense of confidence in his ability to grow and be socially competent because of actual life experiences —not necessarily the worker's interpretation of his feelings or his transference to the worker.

Shattuck's and Martin's article "New Professional Work Roles and Their Integration into a Social Agency Structure" describes how new work roles were found to meet a set of problems in a demonstration program involving the social structure and institutions. In this case the problem was dropping out of school, but it is important to note the general issue that a profession can remain viable only if it remains responsive to new demands. Practitioners have sometimes clung to old methods and have not recognized that different times require different methods and roles. In this instance, as in all practice, the way a problem was perceived determined the methods used.

Because these authors considered the phenomenon of dropping out to be related to the estrangement of the school, they assigned new roles to workers to mediate between the school and parents, to be advocates for their clients with the police, courts, and attendance personnel, and to work with groups of parents to enable them to come to grips with these structural problems. Although the interventions were addressed to the school and related systems, the object was to permit the growth and development of individual students. Any strategy that "keeps something from happening"—like dropping out of school—is preventive intervention; its modes and techniques will derive naturally from the way the case is cast.

CRISIS INTERVENTION

Articles on crisis intervention have been included because this model of practice is an example of an approach taken in behalf of a specialized status of problems, although still useful in examining the framework of preventive intervention. It has other qualities, such as attention to the environment, the emphasis on coping mechanisms, and the goal of helping people master the event, that share some of the purposes and directions suggested in the more general approaches to preventive intervention.

Crisis intervention is possible on the secondary as well as the tertiary level of intervention. The articles in this collection do not discuss practice aimed at reducing stress, broadly defined; that is probably a general aim of all social work practice. Restricting the choice of articles to those dealing with crisis intervention theory was useful for three reasons. (1) Crisis intervention is one of the few predictive theories available in social work. (2) It is one of the few practice models derived from empirical research—in this case, research into specific kinds of crises. (3) It is unique among

available models in its identification of specific steps in intervention that would "keep something from happening." In its technical sense, crisis is most often defined as an imbalance between an objective situational event and the resources or ability of an individual or a group to master that event. This should remind us that cases need not be addressed only at the point of breakdown, after pathological responses appear. The fact that the event might be any extreme situation perceived as a crisis further suggests that the practice model is more heavily influenced by extreme changes in the average, expectable environment than by whether a person is clinically "normal" as measured against a psychosexual standard.

Crises have also been defined as hazardous events that call on new coping capacities in people who perceive special situations as threatening. Such crises may be precipitated by (1) external disasters or events such as illness, (2) transitional states during which it is necessary to make new and untested adaptations such as going to school for the first time or moving, or (3) normal developmental stages such as the onset of puberty or middle age. Increasingly, research has enabled theoreticians and practitioners to define and refine other crisis states and to identify particular implications for intervention. Through improved knowledge, social workers can intervene in potential crisis situations, direct attention to populations-at-risk, specify those steps that enhance the ego-adaptive mechanisms of individuals caught in the pressure of crisis, and invent social supports that will encourage more accommodating and adaptable environments.

Pascwark's and Albers's article "Crisis Intervention: Theory in Search of a Program" is a succinct overview of the types of crises for which intervention procedures have been defined. It discusses stages of crises and suggests implications for practice at each stage. The authors go further than many in this field to connect crisis intervention with secondary and tertiary interventions and show how it is addressed differently in each instance. Their interest in a public health model of practice for community mental health is compelling, and the article should provide the thinking practitioner with unlimited boundaries for creative approaches to prevention.

The remaining five articles illustrate how crisis intervention theory is developing, namely, by addressing a specific crisis event as a field of interaction between a person and situation that requires intervention, most often on the secondary level. Thus Rapoport in another article discusses mothers of premature babies; Fox and Scherl, victims of rape; Oppenheimer, patients with cancer and their families; Blaufarb and Levine, the reaction of parents and children to an earthquake; and Golan and Gruschka, integration of the new immigrant, which reflects some of the characteristics of a transitional state. Each study specifies the interventions that must take place in response to the predictable reactions of the individuals and groups involved in the hazardous states. Whether the actions are related to anticipatory grief, cognitive awareness of the reality of the event, open communication with family members, or exercises in managing immediate tasks in life, the meaning is clear in each article. Preventive intervention demands an active, inventive practitioner, continually seeking effective points for intervention, earlier rather than later, using the client's untapped strength, with the goal of restoring or improving the balance between the person and his environment.

Crisis intervention is presented as one example of preventive intervention, and only because as a theoretical formulation it has a certain clarity and assuredness about it. Countless other examples of preventive in-tervention are taking place in social work and are being described and analyzed in the literature of the behavioral and social sciences. Each time a practitioner participates in the client's field to help set things right before they become hopelessly damaged, there is movement toward "keeping something from happening." Clearly, this mode of practice will change the form and content of the traditional roles of the client and worker and the place in which dysfunction or imbalance is sought. Without question, pursuit of this approach to practice will highlight the growth, development, and change in the ego capacities of clients and will diminish efforts by the worker to track down the etiology of emotional disease or to assume a psychotherapeutic goal or cure.

DIFFERENT GOALS

The differences among theories of preventive intervention and therapy stem from two different goals: that of (1) enhancing the reciprocal adaptations between the person and a situation and (2) seeking changes in personality in accordance with clinically normative criteria. The blurring of the distinctions between these goals of practice interferes with the social worker's effectiveness in preventive intervention. To keep something from happening, it is necessary to recast the way in which we view cases; that is, we must enlarge the unit of attention. Once a case has been defined so it focuses on the transactions of the person in a situation, it is apparent that a person's environment needs to be influenced with the same skill that is applied when we focus on enhancing a person's intellectual, emotional, physical, and social capacities for adaptation. Social work is the proper field for this mode of practice. Its purpose is to enhance social functioning. Its developing knowledge base creates the perspective and the map for it. Clients—all of us—are in various stages of maladaptations with dysfunctional aspects of our personal environments. Social workers are needed while people are still able to cope, rather than when they have become overwhelmed. The design is available—all that is left is the choice.

CAROL H. MEYER, EDITOR

New York, New York
June 1974

BY LYDIA RAPOPORT

The Concept of Prevention in Social Work

Social work is experiencing a rapidly changing emphasis in professional practice. It seeks new knowledge and methodologies. The fluidity of the professional framework makes it especially accommodating to the absorption of new theory and constructs, and causes it to be particularly prone to global identifications with new models, which may or may not fit the abiding purposes and goals of the profession.[1] This problem is exemplified by the current high interest in the concept of prevention in social work practice. It is the thesis of this paper that the concept of prevention, borrowed largely from the public health model, is often used in a distorted and confusing manner in the social work framework.

PROBLEMS OF TERMINOLOGY

Interest in the concept of prevention has been given impetus by several distinct trends. One reason for enhanced interest is an outgrowth of changes within the social work profession itself, particularly in its evolving relationship to society as a whole. Wilensky and Lebeaux have called attention to the

LYDIA RAPOPORT, M.S.S., *is lecturer in social welfare and co-ordinator of field work at the School of Social Welfare, University of California, Berkeley, California. This paper was written when the author was on leave, serving as research associate in community mental health at the Harvard School of Public Health. It was first presented to the Psychiatric Social Work Section of NASW, Eastern Massachusetts Chapter, in June 1960.*

changing emphasis in social work from a "residual function" to an "institutional function."[2] When social work and social welfare are conceived of as a residual agency, they are seen as attending to temporary and emergency problems that arise when the regular and normal need-meeting social institutions break down and fail to provide adequately for basic human needs. In this residual role, social work is primarily concerned with amelioration and direct service methods to relieve stress and social breakdown.

From one point of view this conception represents a mechanistic concept of society and of social welfare, which might be compared to the mechanistic concept of disease. Here, the organism—society—is conceived of as a machine, and disease—social problems—is viewed as a breakdown in one of

[1] This point of view has been stated masterfully by Charlotte Towle: "Among professions social work has had very little stability. It has been continuously in the making and remaking. It has never really had a chance to jell. Its orthodoxies have been relatively weak and its segmentation, as implied in specialization, short-lived. The tempo of its growth, always under necessitous circumstances, disposes it to ready identifications, both as a means to learning and as a defense. It is an avid consumer of nurture afforded. It is vulnerable to new integrations; herein lies its potential for growth or regression." In "Implications of Contemporary Human and Social Values for Selection of Social Work Students," *Social Service Review*, Vol. 33, No. 3 (September 1959), p. 264.

[2] H. L. Wilensky and C. N. Lebeaux, *Industrialization and Social Welfare* (New York: Russell Sage Foundation, 1955), pp. 98–99.

its constituent parts. Faulty parts are then mended or replaced.[3]

The newer conception views social welfare and social work services as regular, ongoing, and essential features of modern industrialized society, in which change in basic institutional patterns is rapid and ever present; welfare provisions and programs are seen as an essential component of modern life, transformed from temporary needs into basic rights. In this model, concern is not with faulty parts or conditions, but with the viability of human response and adaptation.[4] It would seem, then, that this newer concept of welfare as essential and ongoing, and therefore as a more growth-promoting type of institution, is particularly compatible with the philosophy and efforts of prevention.

This newer concept has been articulated in Werner Boehm's paper on the nature of social work.[5] In it he describes the functions of social work as follows:

1. *Restoration*—which consists of removal and control of factors which cause breakdown or impairment of social relationships. This function is essentially curative and rehabilitative.

2. *Provision of resources*—which is concerned with the creation, enrichment, and improvement of social resources. This function is essentially developmental and educational.

3. *Prevention*—which consists of early discovery, control, and elimination of conditions which *potentially* could hamper social functioning. It consists of (a) prevention of problems in the area of interaction between individuals and groups, and (b) prevention of social ills, through the study of "social infection" and "social contamination," and by the function of provision.

Another source of influence arises from our greater knowledge of the expanding field of public health, in which prevention figures as the key concept around which its functions are organized. Because prevention is a central organizing concept for the practice of public health, all its activities are subsumed under the umbrella concept of prevention. However, underneath the big umbrella the activities are strictly and variously defined according to different levels. A commonly accepted conceptualization of the levels of prevention in public health is in accordance with five gradients of activity, stretched along a continuum of what might be called the natural history of disease, including the prepathogenic period. The five levels are grouped as follows: (1) health promotion, (2) specific protection, (3) early diagnosis and treatment, (4) disability limitation, and (5) rehabilitation.[6]

Another frequent and more succinct way of grouping these activities has been in the order of primary, secondary, and tertiary prevention. These terms are heard increasingly in social work and will bear some elaboration.

1. *Primary prevention* includes measures undertaken to obviate the development of disease in susceptible populations. It consists of *health promotion*, which includes all measures and institutions that enhance the general well-being of a population. Primary prevention also encompasses the concept of *specific protection*, which implies some knowledge of causation and consists in the health field of such measures as immunization, sanitation, sound nutrition, and so forth.

---

[3] J. L. Halliday, "Principles of Aetiology," *British Journal of Medical Psychology,* Vol. 19, Parts III and IV (1943), pp. 367–380.

.[4] Sir Geoffrey Vickers, in a paper on "What Sets the Goals of Public Health?" notes that with the introduction of the National Health Service in Great Britain a widespread, if half-conscious, view was held that a health service was a self-limiting service. In actuality, he maintains, the amount of effort that can be devoted to the health of individuals and the community increases indefinitely with scientific developments. *New England Journal of Medicine,* Vol. 258, No. 12 (March 1958), pp. 589–596.

[5] Werner W. Boehm, "The Nature of Social Work," *Social Work,* Vol. 3, No. 2 (April 1958), pp. 16–17.

[6] H. R. Leavell and E. G. Clark, *Preventive Medicine—for the Doctor and His Community* (New York: McGraw-Hill Book Co., 1958), Chap. 2.

2

2. *Secondary prevention* generally encompasses case-finding, diagnosis, and treatment. The emphasis is on *early* diagnosis and treatment. While treatment specifically attends to the relief of distress, as conceived in terms of secondary prevention it seeks to shorten duration, reduce symptoms, limit sequelae, and minimize contagion.

3. *Tertiary prevention* is largely concerned with chronic or irreversible illness; the goals are limitation of disability resulting from the illness and promotion of rehabilitation measures.

We see then that the total range of public health activity has been subsumed under three levels of prevention.

Social work has tended to embrace this model in an undiscriminating fashion, claiming that all social work activities are in the nature of prevention—or at least have preventive components. Such a claim can be made with any pretense at seriousness only if prevention is conceived of as a very relative term. We have already seen that in public health usage the term does reflect the whole of public health activities, but at the same time describes precisely the mediating and intervening steps that can be taken along the continuum of the natural history of disease, including the premorbid phase. In social work, the continuum may be along (1) a time dimension or (2) in accordance with the degree of pathological involvement. Thus we tend to call any intervention "prevention" if it is taken earlier rather than later (the philosophy of the "whole child" guidance movement rests on this view). Catching a disorder at the time of onset is considered prevention; if dealt with later it becomes treatment. This time dimension does not make for precision in theory or practice.

The other continuum is laid out on the axis of degree of pathology—*i.e.*, mild to serious. Intervention at a point of mild disturbance is considered prevention, insofar as the expectation is that a more serious or chronic state will be forestalled. In actuality, all these intervening activities occur *after* the existence of a defined problem—mild or serious, early or late—and therefore are examples of secondary or tertiary prevention.

We shall consider next the problem posed by the document, *Prevention and Treatment,* prepared by the NASW Commission on Practice, Subcommittee on Trends, Issues, and Priorities.[7] The issues are clearly presented, but the conclusions are ambivalent.

PROBLEMS OF DEFINITION

The statement affirms that we need clarity regarding the conceptualization of prevention in social work in order to stimulate and give impetus to preventive functions. It notes that "if prevention were regarded as inclusive of practically all social work practice functions and activities, the concept could easily become watered down and might well lose its *distinctive contribution* [italics supplied]." [8] The hope is that out of clarity will come new areas for exploration and emphasis in regard to their preventive possibilities. Hence clarity of definition is sought as a means of strengthening strategy. The search is for a concept of prevention likely to result in the greatest stimulus to a newer and effective practice.

This clear and affirmative position is abandoned as the statement struggles to gain recognition for the myriad social work interventions that are part of our broad treatment methods, by trying to make them part of prevention or to recognize in them a preventive component. All social work activities here are dedicated to the proposition that a condition must be kept from getting worse. The objective is sound, but why do such endeavors have to be dignified with the preventive label? In this instance, treatment and prevention become coterminous and we are right back where we started. Preventing an increase in severity or spread

7 By Bertram M. Beck, based on the subcommittee's work, January 1959. (Mimeographed.)

8 *Ibid.*, p. 9.

3

is more aptly called "control." This is a good and clear concept, but the NASW statement maintains regretfully that if the role of social work is the control of social problems, this leaves it without a preventive role.[9]

The statement then considers whether to narrow down the scope of prevention to apply to situations which are not now, but threaten to become, pathological. One is therefore dealing with potential rather than actual problems, or with pathology in its *earlier* stages. Here the statement hedges again: by combining potential problems with early pathology, primary prevention is made out to be coextensive with secondary prevention, which is concerned with case-finding and early treatment.

The final statement points to the fundamental ambivalence. The drafters of the document, we are told, discarded the possibility of defining prevention in a restricted sense as meaning "keeping something from happening." [10] The reason for this astonishing conclusion is that practically all social work activities are launched after a problem is manifest. The logic embedded in this decision is questionable: since the narrow definition of prevention excludes most of present social work, it is proposed that we discard the narrow definition and label what we are now traditionally doing as "prevention." The implications are worrisome indeed; they directly negate the earlier stated purpose to find a definition that will give the greatest impetus to newer modes of approach. The discarded definition is the most likely to yield fresh and creative social work activities.

From the above discussion the question arises as to whether there is any validity in altering social work language in order to dignify our traditional efforts with a more popular term. This is mere sophistry and turns a word into a slogan. What we are doing is to take the word "prevention" out of the more precise public health context and apply it to the social work field, whose rationale, objectives, and methodologies cannot all be neatly squeezed into a single organizing concept. To strive to apply a unitary organizing concept to a field that operates by many others—and in any case has not reached consensus or stability as to what this concept shall be—only creates confusion, leads to unsubstantiated claims and professional self-deception, and fails to further our purposes either scientifically or professionally.

The struggle to encompass the concept of prevention is reminiscent of the profession's struggle to define rehabilitation. There we vacillated from defining rehabilitation as a point of view, or approach, to the narrower conception of a specific type of endeavor conducted in a medical facility concerned with restoration of physical and social functioning. The controversy has largely abated. In general, there is merit in defining an area of practice more narrowly in order to improve professional practice.

PROBLEMS OF "MYTHOLOGY"

The next group of problems to be discussed deal with implicit value assumptions. Some approach the order of myths and serve as determinants as to what position we take.

One view of the concept and objectives of prevention is embedded in an ideal value assumption which elevates prevention to the top of any hierarchy in a continuum of health and welfare activities. Thus the assertion is made that prevention of the development and spread of social pathology is better than amelioration, cure,[11] or rehabilitation of such ills. If this means that

---

[9] *Ibid.,* p. 12.
[10] *Ibid.,* p. 9.

[11] The notion of cure in the realm of social pathology and even in defined psychiatric illness is itself a fiction, since it contains the idea of an absolute state of health; the archaic term for "cure" is "heal," which—despite its religious or mystical aura —is closer to our purposes. This implies restoration to soundness, which is more compatible with current ideas of restoration of functioning. Similarly, Dr. Mary Sarvis suggests that psychotherapies are largely based on the surgical model of excision instead of being flexibly based on the "useful next step."

the possibility of sparing people suffering, distress, or unwholesome experiences is a worthy objective, then the value position is an incontrovertible one from any humanitarian or professional standpoint. If, however, it means that applying measures to relieve any one given individual from distress or destructive experience is less worthy than the application of broad social measures to relieve suffering in general—then, for social work, this is an indefensible position. For deeply in the core of the social work profession's value base rests the assumption that the highest good is the protection and preservation of the essential worth, dignity, and integrity of each and any human being. This essential value is more central to our profession than any other, and has led social work to give at least equal if not more attention to the psychological meaning and human impact of the helping process itself, rather than to development of helping techniques alone.

Another myth is the notion that the task of working at the preventive level is easier, less frustrating, and more rewarding as to results than trying to intervene at the level of manifest and well-developed pathology, which may be highly complex, entrenched, and even irreversibly chronic. There is little evidence to warrant such a belief. In the realm of social pathology the problems of definition and intervention are equally complex, given the present state of our knowledge, regardless of the level of prevention. Moreover, we are not yet in a position to assert which level of activities yields the greatest gains in terms of effectiveness. As a matter of fact, some hold the opinion that, since prevention in social work is a new, untried, and fuzzy area, we at least have greater certainty of results—even within familiar limitations of resources, skills, size of population reached, and so forth—with known methods of treatment and rehabilitation.

The NASW statement raises the question of the relationship of prevention to social change. The statement expresses the concern that if social work were to move toward heavier emphasis on prevention, "the profession might lose sight of its major role as an inducer of social change." [12] The reasoning behind this remarkable concern seems to be as follows: positive changes in society often induce social problems as a result of a process of social change. Social work does not wish to reduce social change in order to reduce social problems. Moreover, it recognizes that problems of disordered individuals and groups may arise in part from a discord between them and social norms. Social work therefore has a role in inducing social change in order to deal with unhealthy social norms. Prevention in social work is seen as being directed to social change and to individuals and groups whose problems are induced by social change and by conflict with social norms.

All this is quite reasonable and in keeping with professional objectives and commitments. However, the following question is then addressed to the membership in the statement of issues: "Can social work prevent problems from arising and still escape the role of being an instrument to induce conformity?" [13] It is not clear how this concluding question evolved out of the foregoing considerations. The goals of prevention and the goals of social change appear somehow made out to be antithetical rather than identical. Perhaps there is an implicit assumption that one can prevent only if one can hold static the variable of social change, which in itself continually produces the germs of new disorders and problems. The statement fails to recognize that preventive activities themselves are generally vehicles for social change.

The above confusing position may be grounded in the initial pronouncement of the NASW statement, which affirms that "social work interest in prevention arises out of the profession's service commitment." [14] This position might be ques-

---

[12] *Op. cit.,* p. 2.
[13] *Ibid.,* p. 4.
[14] *Ibid.,* p. 1.

5

tioned. Furthermore, this major premise may be the cause of some of the above confusions and casuistries. The social work interest in prevention should arise out of the profession's commitment to social change, which the statement has already affirmed to be one of its major roles! If this were declared as the central position, the rest would flow logically and naturally, without any artificial dualism. Moreover, such a position would lead us to explore and concentrate more vigorously on primary prevention as a means of social change, rather than manipulating and stretching concepts of secondary and tertiary prevention which more clearly express the service and ameliorative functions.

One other myth that generates opposing viewpoints should be examined. This is the myth of causation. It is generally posed in the following terms: in order to prevent the onset or spread of a disorder, it is necessary to know the specific factors of causation. This is offered as an argument particularly in the realm of mental illness and in social pathology. Since there is lack of agreement and uncertainty as to specific cause, and increasing recognition of the multicausal nature of these problems, there tends to be a feeling of helplessness or discouragement, if not outright indifference, to the possibilities of prevention. Sometimes, too, the discouragement is managed more distantly by hiding behind the assertion that we need much more research and specific knowledge before we can do anything.

This position is easy to recognize but less than sound from several points of view. In social work we shall always operate with less than full and certain knowledge.[15] This

is one of our built-in professional stresses.[16] Because of the mandate given to us by society and because of the nature of our social commitment, we cannot afford to wait. This is another value position that binds us.

A more cogent argument, however, lies in the nature of the fallacy itself. René Dubos presents the case most lucidly.[17] He points out that modern medicine is wedded to the "doctrine of specific etiology," adopted from the field of infectious diseases and the germ theory of disease from which the bulk of modern medical achievements stem. Until late in the nineteenth century, disease had been regarded as resulting from a lack of harmony between the sick person and his environment. Dr. Dubos points out that the doctrine of specific etiology appeared to negate this philosophical view of health as equilibrium. It did, however, save medicine from a morass of loose words and vague concepts. The theory held that each disease had a well-defined cause and that its control could best be achieved by attacking the causative agent or focusing treatment on the affected part of the body. Dr. Dubos maintains that the present generation actually believes that the control of infectious diseases can be credited to the widespread use of antibacterial drugs. Actually, the mortality of many other infectious diseases began to recede long before the discovery of specific treatment—indeed, before discovery of the germ theory of disease. He credits actual control to the campaigns of humanitarian movements which were dedicated to eradicating the social evils of the industrial revolution and to the restoration of harmony in life with the ways of

[15] A similar position is taken by Dr. B. Pasamanick, a public health psychiatrist, who says, ". . . a considerable amount of prevention and control of mental disorders has occurred, and it would be possible to do prodigiously more in the immediate future without any accumulation of new knowledge of etiology or treatment, provided we are willing to pay the costs in terms of money and social effort." He elaborates further, "The experimental testing of

prevention and control measures may very well open new paths of etiology, and in chronic disorders is frequently the only method for obtaining definitive evidence of causation." From "Prevention and Control of Chronic Disease," *Journal of Public Health*, Vol. 49, No. 9 (September 1959), p. 1129.

[16] L. Rapoport, "In Defense of Social Work: An Analysis of Stress in the Profession," *Social Service Review*, Vol. 34, No. 1 (March 1960).

[17] *The Mirage of Health*, World Perspectives (New York: Harper & Brothers, 1959).

nature. He concludes that it is a remarkable fact that the greatest strides in health improvement were achieved in the field of diseases that responded to social and economic reforms after industrialization.

The implications of this line of thought are so important that they bear restatement by quoting directly from the essay:

> The ancient concept of disharmony between the sick person and his environment seems very primitive and obscure indeed when compared with the precise terminology and explanation of modern medical science.
>
> Unquestionably the doctrine of specific etiology has been the most constructive force in medical research for almost a century and the theoretical and practical achievements to which it has led constitute the bulk of modern medicine. Yet few are the cases in which it has provided a complete account of the causation of disease. Despite frantic efforts, the causes of cancer, of arteriosclerosis, of mental disorders, and of the other great medical problems of our times remain undiscovered. It is generally assumed . . . that the cause of all diseases can and will be found in due time—by bringing the big guns of science to bear on the problems. In reality, however, search for *the* cause may be a hopeless pursuit because most disease states are the indirect outcome of a constellation of circumstances rather than the direct result of single determinant factors.
>
> . . . there are many cases in which a given disease can be controlled by several unrelated procedures.[18]

IMPLICATIONS FOR PRACTICE

The implications are profound in their direct relevance to prevention in social work practice. They suggest strongly that the preoccupation with tracking down a causative agent is far from fruitful or even necessary when dealing with a multifactorial system. It is more useful, therefore, to understand the interrelated parts of a complex system and to plan strategy which could in-

18 *Ibid.,* pp. 86–87.

terrupt, at any one of several points, factors contributing to the development of pathology. Classification of cause into predisposing, precipitating, and perpetuating cause is also useful.

Let us return now to a further examination of some key operating concepts from the field of public health to see how they might be applied in the context of social and emotional health.

1. The major mode of inquiry for public health is the epidemiological method, which studies the incidence and prevalence of a disease and the related factors that seem to be associated with it in a defined population. The use of this method is only in its infancy in the area of mental illness and social pathology, but despite methodological difficulties promises to be very useful as a guide to preventive action.

2. Prevention in public health is directed at the community or a given population and not at specific individuals. Moreover, the population designated for a preventive program is usually a specially selected one, deemed particularly vulnerable to certain hazards, and is thus sometimes designated as "a population at risk."

3. Prevention is carried out via three major types of intervention: (a) removal of the etiological agent; (b) removal of, or altering, one or more important associated factors; and (c) strengthening populations (individuals) against the noxious agent, or related factors. Translated into social-psychological language, this means: (a) removing or diminishing specific stress; (b) reducing the secondary effects of stress; and (c) strengthening the maturational processes and adaptive mechanisms in a population. If these activities are carried out prior to the onset of defined pathology, they are in the nature of primary prevention.[19]

With these concepts in mind, let us examine now where along the continuum of public health prevention we can place social

19 Suggested by unpublished comments of Dr. Leonard J. Duhl, who is with the National Institute of Mental Health.

7

work functions, and what activities in social work practice might readily and profitably be developed in order to enlarge the preventive role. Social work has long been concerned with (1) removal of the stress of deprivation, (2) alleviation of the effects of stress, and (3) strengthening of individuals, achieved through the provision of basic needs and the strengthening of ego-adaptive mechanisms. In general, however, the population for which social work plans its programs and services is one already designated as pathological. Using again the framework developed by Drs. Leavell and Clark, we might say that the bulk of social work activity falls therefore into the category of secondary and tertiary prevention. In Werner Boehm's terminology, this area is covered by the concepts of restoration and, in part, provision. All these measures are relevant to the effort of control of the extent, severity, and spread of social problems. It was suggested earlier that primary prevention—i.e., "keeping something from happening," which was unfortunately discarded by the NASW statement as an operationally useful definition—might, in fact, be the most challenging and creative area in which social work wisdom could be employed and a "distinctive contribution" made. Prevention in its archaic usage meant "to anticipate." Efforts at primary prevention in the realm of social problems is largely in the nature of "presumptive prevention." Nonetheless, our presumptions rest on considerable research and on cumulative empirical wisdom. What, then, are the opportunities for social work in primary prevention?

PRIMARY PREVENTION IN SOCIAL WORK

The first phase of primary prevention is health promotion or, more broadly, promotion of well-being. The whole of society and all its growth-promoting social institutions play a key role here. The family, the field of education, church, organized recre-ation, and so on, are highly relevant. The chief responsibility of social work does not lie in the area of promotion of well-being, although many social workers are directly involved in growth-promoting activities and institutions. An important role of social work, however, might be that of "watch-dog": to be alert to weaknesses or failures in the growth-promoting type of agency—to point them out, and suggest modifications in both specific program and institutional arrangements which may, by their existing nature, defeat the stated objectives. Social work has not been sufficiently articulate in this area. We are beginning, however, to develop interest in, and more specific knowledge about, the impact of institutional arrangements and culture on personality development.

Social work could also be instrumental in encouraging the health- and welfare-promoting agencies to develop programs which would strengthen individuals in dealing with specific life tasks. Efforts could be directed at maturational processes and adaptive mechanisms. This is sometimes referred to as "emotional immunization," which—analogous to physical immunization—can be passively or actively acquired. Passive immunization in mental health is acquired through the elimination, or more realistically the reduction, of stress. Active immunity can be promoted by strengthening people in methods of problem-solving through information, training, and experience as a way of preparation for dealing with unanticipated crises, as well as crises of maturational steps and role transition. For example, family life education could be directed more sharply at younger, less emotionally competent groups as preparation for husband-wife roles and later parent roles, including preparation for parental tasks and expectation of child development and nurture. Some of this, called "anticipatory guidance," is being done increasingly with individuals who make use of the secondary prevention type of program. It should also be done with populations not

8

yet manifesting problems, which can be predicted as likely to develop difficulties.[20]

The second phase of primary prevention, that of specific protection, is a most challenging area in which to apply social work knowledge and skills. Several different types of activity come to mind. One is the social work function of provision, which Werner Boehm rightly considers as having a role in prevention and which could be classified in the second step of primary prevention, that of specific protection. Thus the intent of the social security program is to offer specific protection to a population at large against the stress of basic deprivations through income loss.

Another example is that of Dr. John Bowlby's studies of the effects of prolonged and early maternal separation and maternal deprivation. These studies yield data and guides for action toward specific protection. All measures that would reduce the incidence of maternal separation would be a form of specific protection. The absence of a continuing and satisfactory mothering relationship is presumed, on fairly good evidence, to lead to the development of psychopathology, and repeated and prolonged separations are presumed to lead specifically toward the development of psychopathy—what Dr. Bowlby used to call the "affectionless character." The measures already taken along the lines of specific protection are increased parental visiting in pediatric hospitals, increased home treatment, homemakers at time of crisis to keep children from being placed, modification of adoption laws and procedures to facilitate earlier adoption, and so forth. Social work contributes to change in this area through the active use of existing services and by recommending administrative and legal modifications.

Still another approach is exemplified in a pediatric hospital project.[21] This program is designed to protect children from the effects of separation, isolation, and specific reaction to medical and surgical procedures. The method used is that of social group work and consists of guided group experiences, catharsis through verbalization and play, and the opportunity for mastery of traumatic events as well as growth-oriented experiences. Intervention here is beamed at a particularly vulnerable population, *i.e.,* groups of children in the hospital. It is directed at lowering the hazards encountered in a hospital by provision of a direct service to groups of children and by influencing ward management and procedures (the institution) in order to strengthen the children's adaptive and growth potential.

Much more could be done in the area of specific protection by way of reducing the secondary effects of stress, in this instance the stress of separation for the young child. For example, we might become more alert to the remarkable increase in the number of working mothers of young children for whom continued and adequate nurture is required, not only at family crisis points, but as a style of life in which separation and substitute mothering become a daily reality. We have done very little to provide adequate day care services as part of public social policy, and even less to build into day care programs all the mental health safeguards and services with which we are already familiar and which we could offer as methods of specific protection.

There is another role for social work which needs urgent expansion, viz., the re-evaluation and reorganization of health and welfare services with some of the following objectives:

1. To help people get needed service at the time of acute need with a minimum of the administrative obstacles that tend to eliminate all but the most highly motivated or most chronically dependent. For example, the ever lengthening waiting lists of

---

[20] *See* a challenging paper by Jessie Bernard, "Neomarital Programs," in which she uses the concept of "anticipatory socialization." *The Social Welfare Forum, 1958* (New York: Columbia University Press, 1958), pp. 239–255.

[21] At Boston City Hospital, under the social work direction of Marion Chuan.

child guidance clinics, and now increasingly of family agencies, make a mockery of the need for early and prompt treatment (secondary prevention). One may question the necessity of formal and lengthy diagnostic studies on a routine basis which may or may not be of real consequence to a family, and which often fail to be shared in a vital fashion with appropriate caretakers who could conceivably, with consultation, be of assistance to the family.

2. To insure that services are offered in a manner which does not tend to fragment the individual or the family, but takes into its purview the total person and family need. For example, in settings where social work is an auxiliary service it becomes particularly important to bring this point of view to other professions. In such settings, social work serves to reduce fragmentation by co-ordinating resources with need.

3. To guard against legal structure and administrative usage which, in actuality if not by intent, undermine and impair the independent striving of individuals and put a premium on regressive and passive tendencies. For example, one might question whether the regulations and administration of certain social security programs do in fact enhance independent functioning or whether they unwittingly reinforce dependency. There is evidence that some of the built-in strictures of the medical disability program and the Aid to Dependent Children program tend to undermine certain healthy strivings and reinforce certain forms of personal and family disorganization.[22]

In summary, the point of view here urged is that social work has major responsibility for amelioration and control, and a vital role in all levels of prevention. Prevention should be more strictly defined to sharpen professional practice and give impetus to greater activity in the area of primary prevention, which involves the imaginative application of all social work methods in anticipating problems and needs.

[22] For further elucidation of this problem see Alvin L. Schorr, "Problems in the ADC Program," *Social Work*, Vol. 5, No. 2 (April 1960).

BY MAX SIPORIN

Social Treatment: A New-Old Helping Method

■ *As part of social work's response to the current social needs of individuals and families, there has been a reemergence and revitalization of social treatment as a helping method for the provision of direct services. The author describes the rediscoveries as well as innovative developments of operational concepts and procedures that express social work perspectives of the earlier and current social reform eras.* ■

MAJOR CHANGES IN social work method have taken place in recent years as part of the social work profession's response to the crises and upheavals of our time. These changes have resulted in the emergence of professional modes of helping services that have important points of similarity with those of an earlier era of social reform.

From 1892 to 1917, and especially at the beginning of this century, the new profession of social work emphasized social legislative action, social institutional reform, and broad preventive programs as its preferred methods of practice. However, there was also a climate of opinion within certain social work circles that depreciated direct services to individuals and family groups. As Richmond later recalled, she was one of

MAX SIPORIN, DSW, *is Professor, School of Social Welfare, State University of New York at Albany, Albany, New York. A shortened version of this paper was presented at the Annual Meeting of the Maryland Chapter of the National Association of Social Workers, Baltimore, Maryland, June 12, 1969. The author expresses appreciation to his former casework students and faculty colleagues at the School of Social Work, University of Maryland, Baltimore, Maryland, who participated in an analysis of current and emerging social work practice with individuals and families on which this paper is partly based.*

the caseworkers who were "often waved aside as having outlived [their] usefulness" because "legislation and propaganda, between them, would render social work with and for individuals unnecessary." [1]

At this same time, though, there was a remarkable and common development, within both the Charity Organization Societies and the social settlements, of a social work helping method for use with individuals and families. It was variously called charity work, scientific philanthropy, friendly visiting, social casework, or social treatment. Of course the method that came to be known mostly as social casework had a long history. But it was during this social reform period that it gained a distinctive identity. It became a way of providing a wide range of individualized services in what today might be called a multifunctional set of procedures. The method evolved at a time when social workers were less fragmented and more unified in their helping approaches. They had a broad, idealistic yet realistic vision of serving the individual and society. They sought to aid the individual as a social being and the family as a social unit and thus help create

[1] Mary E. Richmond, *The Long View* (New York: Russell Sage Foundation, 1930), p. 586.

a new social order in which poverty and ill health could be prevented. The method they fashioned was highly conceptual and creative. It continued to have a great vitality in practice and in the development of practice theory during the 1920s and thereafter.

This methodological orientation suffered a decline in usefulness and popularity after 1917, when many social workers committed themselves to individual moral reform and psychoanalytic forms of therapy. It is indeed fortunate that in recent years the older, more traditional, larger conception of the social work helping method has been rediscovered and found relevant for current needs. There has been a rapid and exciting renewal of its development in social work practice and education. It is being referred to again as social treatment and also as comprehensive casework or clinical social work.

In this paper the concept and characteristics of social treatment will be examined both from a historical point of view and as they seem to be unfolding today. This discussion is based in large part on an analysis of current and emerging social work practice with individuals and families carried out by the author and his students. In examining practice and the relevant literature, there was a particular concern to determine how a problem-task focus is changing the patterns of helping procedures used by social workers in clinical practice; for example, in regard to the problems of alienated poverty, juvenile delinquency, child abuse and neglect, vocational maladjustment, psychosis, and marital conflict. What follows, then, is both a charting of current changes and a foreshadowing of new and needed developments in direct social work services to individuals and family groups.

THE CONCEPT

The term "social treatment" was used by many social workers prior to World War I and during the 1920s to mean social case treatment and social casework as well as to refer to its action-change aspect. Witmer observed that during the "social reform era of social work," social treatment was conceived largely in terms of the organization and coordination of community resources, so that social casework had a "community organization aspect." [2] It included family rehabilitation efforts as well as aid to individuals. This was the period when the procedures of what came to be called group work and community organization had not yet been separated out as specialized methods, but were part of a natural way by which one helped individuals and families. The social casework method as practiced before 1917 is described as having been family centered and as "group work with families." [3]

For Richmond, social treatment complemented social diagnosis as one of the two basic components of "social casework," a term she had resisted and did not care for. [4] She regarded social treatment as a "combination of services" through which "readjustments" were made within the individual and the social environment through "re-education of habits," "the influence of mind upon mind," and changes in the network of social relationships among family members, friends, neighbors, religious congregations, schools, and so forth. Lee held that social treatment should incorporate financial relief programs; he later explicated this method as helping individuals and families through "executive" procedures (managing

[2] Helen L. Witmer, *Social Work* (New York: Farrar & Rinehart, 1942), pp. 161–180.

[3] Bertha C. Reynolds, "Rethinking Social Casework," *Social Work Today*, Vol. 5, No. 4 (April 1938), pp. 5–8; No. 5 (May 1938), pp. 5–7; No. 6 (June 1938), pp. 5–8.

[4] Mary E. Richmond, *What is Social Case Work?* (New York: Russell Sage Foundation, 1922), pp. 90, 108–112, and 122. On her preference for the term "friendly visiting" over that of "social casework," see *The Long View*, p. 97.

a service program) and "leadership" (relationship-motivational) procedures.[5]

This enlarged and wide-ranging conception of method was underlined by a number of social work leaders. Abbott, for example, spoke of social treatment (meaning social casework) as a "broad field [containing] the whole science of human relations," rather than limiting it to the specialized procedures of psychiatric social work.[6] In the Milford Conference report in 1929 social treatment was viewed as blending in a generic way the content of the social casework "specializations" that had arisen by that time.[7]

Despite the increasing dominance of the psychoanalytic point of view, there was a continued development of ideas about social treatment that amplified Richmond's conceptualization. Sheffield urged a "situational approach" in social casework in which "group adjustive" and "social learning" processes, involving changes in social perceptions and social relationships, could aid personal maturation and "family re-education."[8] Reynolds emphasized the sociopsychological bonds between client and community and the need for environmental change to meet clients' needs.[9]

Young presented social treatment as "a method of social therapy" for the juvenile delinquent that would achieve

. . . not only changes in his habits and

reactions but changes in the social relations which he maintains with his family, school and other groups, changes in the community and its institutions.[10]

She also considered treatment primarily a "reconditioning" and "re-education process," and, like Sheffield, gave prominence to "redefinition of the situation." This method included the "services of many professionals and resources," as well as the treatment of the family group and family life education about housekeeping and "child-training" practices.

In this perspective there was a remarkable interest in social processes and group dynamics, in emergent social values and purposes. Thus Richmond became enthusiastic about the new "small group psychology" that would provide a "stronger technique" for social treatment.[11] Reynolds sought to revive the direct social reformist intentions of the earlier period of practice. Lindeman conceived of "social therapeutics" as a form of social work practice in which "the forms of social organization" are adjusted "to produce cohesion among the constituent units, and the individuals . . . adjusted to the social forms without sacrificing their essential freedom."[12] This kind of procedural orientation was well expressed by Young, who sharply differentiated social treatment from psychotherapeutic casework:

Social therapy means linking the person to the structure and function of the social group which influences him, sustains him, and at the same time requires his support, cooperation, and the sharing of responsibilities for the common wealth . . . . It promotes the inherent social impulses

[5] Porter R. Lee, *Social Work as Cause and Function* (New York: Columbia University Press, 1937), pp. 39 and 191–199.

[6] Edith Abbott, *Social Welfare and Professional Education* (2d ed.; Chicago: University of Chicago Press, 1942), pp. 48–49.

[7] *Social Case Work: Generic and Specific* (New York: American Association of Social Workers, 1929).

[8] Ada E. Sheffield, *Social Insight in Case Situations* (New York: Appleton-Century Co., 1937).

[9] *See* Reynolds, op. cit.; and Reynolds, "Between Client and Community," *Smith College Studies in Social Work*, Vol. 5, No. 1 (September 1934), pp. 5–138.

[10] Pauline V. Young, *Social Treatment Probation and Delinquency* (New York: McGraw-Hill Book Co., 1937), p. 290.

[11] Richmond, *The Long View*, pp. 484–491.

[12] Eduard C. Lindeman, "From Social Work to Social Science," in Robert Gessner, ed., *The Democratic Man* (Boston: Beacon Press, 1956), p. 208.

3

of human beings and releases their energies for activity and service. Integration and participation in group life on a democratic basis creates that "wider social self" which tends to make life meaningful and useful. The socialized person tends to accept responsibility not only for himself but for others. . . . he tends to develop a social philosophy of life. . . . In short, mobilization of the latent powers of the family and group cooperating in full strength is one of the basic social techniques in aiding the person and the family to aid themselves and others.[13]

The social therapists were, however, out of tune with the prevailing Freudian ethic and the preoccupation with effecting personality change through psychological procedures. Virginia Robinson, Charlotte Towle, Gordon Hamilton, and others helped to redirect social caseworkers toward a psychotherapeutic ideology. The term social treatment fell into disuse and was replaced by references to the limited procedures of "environmental manipulation."[14]

Today the revived term social treatment is again an attempt to distinguish a pattern of direct service quite different from psychotherapeutic casework. There are certain negative connotations about alternative rubrics, such as comprehensive casework and clinical social work, that are avoided by the older term. In the social treatment approach the therapeutic objectives of personality growth and change remain of central importance, but they are regarded as inextricably bound up with and conditioned by social environmental structures and changes, particularly in family and community situations. The return to the concept of social treatment marks a major shift back to traditional perspectives, to a concern with person and situation, family and community values, and socially progressive purposes and processes.

THE METHOD

Social treatment may be defined as a general method for helping individuals and family groups cope with their social problems and improve their social functioning. The scope and boundary of this method are determined by the focus of attention and effort on direct assistance to individuals and family groups, with their individualized problems and functioning.[15] This is in contrast to interventive programs aimed at helping to change neighborhood groups, social organizations, communities, or social welfare institutions to improve their corporate functioning. It has been fallacious to consider the casework method as being limited to one-to-one relationships between the social worker and client. This limitation forced therapeutic purposes to become narrow, fragmentary, and therefore inadequate for the attainment of needed objectives.

To help people with their social problems the systematic, skilled implementation of an extensive repertoire of specific, concrete procedures and resources, of powerful ways and means, is required. Traditionally these procedures consist of assessment, planning, implementation, evaluative feedback, corrective, and continued action activities. The intention is to assert influence through such procedures and processes so as to effect desired change in individuals, social environments, or, usually, in both systems and

---

[13] Pauline V. Young, *Social Case Work in National Defense* (New York: Prentice-Hall, 1941), p. 215.

[14] Gordon Hamilton, *Theory and Practice of Social Casework* (2d ed.; New York: Columbia University Press, 1951), pp. 246–249.

[15] Method as used here refers to purposeful, instrumental activity—an orderly use of means and procedures—including the application of knowledge, attitudes, and skills to accomplish tasks and achieve goals. As Buchler explains, it is "a power of purposive manipulation in a specific recognizable form and order of activity . . . a reproducible order of utterance . . . a tangled cluster of doings, makings and assertings." Justus Buchler, *The Concept of Method* (New York: Columbia University Press, 1961), pp. 135–144.

4

in the relationships between them.[16] The social treatment method thus consists of interventive procedures in which the social worker uses relationships with individuals, families, small groups, organizations, milieus, and communities and intervenes purposefully, adequately, and effectively in these systems to help individuals and families resolve their problems. Psychotherapy is but one set of procedures within the method of social treatment.

It is now recognized that many social workers in direct service use interventions that have been thought of as casework, group work, or community organization procedures.[17] But as Meyer has well asserted: "The traditional separation of casework, group work and community organization is no longer tenable."[18] Such an approach implies a rejection of ritualistic, methodical activism and a deemphasis on method in the sense of a "methodolatry" that lacks regard for aims and results.[19] Social treatment calls for a focus on the problems, goals, and tasks to which method is addressed.

PROBLEM-PERSON-SITUATION MODEL

Social treatment also represents a return to the problem-person-situation model that has been the basic, traditional model for casework.[20] It was Richmond who articu-

lated this theoretical structure when she defined social diagnosis as the identification of the "social difficulty" (or "social need") of the human being and of his social situation.[21] What has also been referred to as the person-in-situation perspective was further developed by Cannon and Klein, Sheffield, Reynolds, Young, and Hamilton and was recently restated by Hollis.[22] It is a definite theoretical framework that was in large part abandoned when social work became preoccupied with psychodynamics and psychopathology.

This traditional model offers a more suitable alternative to the medical symptom-illness view of social problems. Furthermore, it clarifies and emphasizes the concepts of problem and situation (as distinguished from the concept of personality) more than does psychotherapeutic casework. The psychosocial problems of clients are now better understood as difficulties in social functioning and social relationships, as social disability and deviant behavior. They are therefore reactions to and outcomes of maladjustive transactional processes between person and situation, not properties of a person or situation.[23]

The traditional framework can now be understood as representing a systems model based on three interdependent, interacting elements: problem, person, and situation. Such a gestalt exhibits systemic, structural, functional, and change characteristics. Causality becomes a matter of a system's structure and part relationships, rather than of individual responsibility and blame.

[16] See Richmond, *The Long View*, p. 576; Hamilton, *op. cit.*, p. 239; and "Working Definition of Social Work Practice," in Harriett M. Bartlett, "Toward Clarification and Improvement of Social Work Practice," *Social Work*, Vol. 3, No. 2 (April 1958), pp. 3–9.

[17] Harriett M. Bartlett, "Characteristics of Social Work," *Building Social Work Knowledge* (New York: National Association of Social Workers, 1964), pp. 1–15.

[18] Carol H. Meyer, "The Changing Concept of Individualized Services," *Social Casework*, Vol. 47, No. 5 (May 1966), pp. 279–285.

[19] Buchler, op. cit., pp. 105–106.

[20] See Bernece K. Simon, "Borrowed Concepts: Problems and Issues for Curriculum Planning," *Health and Disability Concepts in Social Work Education* (Minneapolis: School of Social Work, University of Minnesota, 1964), pp. 31–41.

[21] Mary E. Richmond, *Social Diagnosis* (New York: Russell Sage Foundation, 1917), p. 62.

[22] M. Antoinette Cannon and Philip Klein, eds., *Social Casework: An Outline for Teaching* (New York: Columbia University Press, 1933); and Florence Hollis, *Casework: Psychosocial Therapy* (New York: Random House, 1964).

[23] A situation is a segment of the social environment that has meaning for the individual and refers to some social group in focused action at a certain time and place. Person-situation relationships become a focus for interventive effort, particularly for personality and identity change.

Behavior becomes problematic and deviant when defined as dysfunctional for the system's needs. Social workers are pulled away from a predilection for intrapsychic conflict issues, and resources become important elements for input-outcome relations.

From such a wide and holistic viewpoint, it is easier to see that interventive change in one variable of the system affects its other parts and thus affects the equilibrium and functioning of the whole. This means that strategic intervention has wide, amplifying consequences, as was noted by the pioneer social workers.[24] The systemic character of social treatment thus calls for a comprehensiveness in the helping approach and a concern with both dysfunctional personality and social system, with interactive personal and group objectives and tasks that will affect the parts and the whole of the case gestalt. Especially important is the need for feedback information loops and a self-monitoring kind of self-awareness to enable self-corrective, goal-directed interventive behavior.

The problem-person-situation model, because of its complex and multifactorial character, compels social workers to seek out and make use of a variety of theories and the interventive approaches, strategies, and programs derived from them. Thus we find ourselves applying relevant aspects of theories about social problems and deviant behavior; adapting personality change approaches based on psychoanalytic, behavioral learning, and humanistic-existentialist theories; and implementing social-situational change approaches based on theories about social situations and groups and marital, family, milieu, organizational, community, and welfare systems. Each of these

theories offers some mode of response to different aspects of therapeutic tasks. Practice "theory" needs to be eclectic and must evolve integrative links for the operational use of personality and social system theories, such as propositions about deviant behavior, role, identity, social situation, crisis, and conflict resolution. It would appear that during the past quarter of a century social workers have unknowingly evolved an integrative framework of personality and situational change procedures under the guise of "crisis therapy," whose principles seem to be applicable in both short-term and long-term interventive programs with individuals and family groups.

Within the context of social treatment the concepts of diagnosis and treatment take on different connotations and operational procedures. There is a greater tendency to apply phenomenological perspectives in understanding the social situation and the subjective world of the client as he experiences them. There is an explicit *assessment of the social situation,* including an appraisal of the structural adequacy and functional efficiency of the family and other groups, organizations, and communities in which the client is an active member. Social workers find that they are again more directly concerned with the assessment of work-employment situations and the vocational functioning of clients and that they actually do much vocational counseling without recognizing that it has remained a basic function for social workers in many settings.

Social workers are more interested now in *personality assessment* that emphasizes the sociopsychological, interactional aspects of personality. This requires them to evaluate and help individuals with their self-concepts and self-esteem, which are related to social, personal, and self-identities; social skills and interpersonal competence; and social learning and social reinforcement processes. There is a growing conviction about the validity of social work's charac-

---

24 *See,* for example, Richmond, *What is Social Casework?* pp. 136–139. For a helpful discussion of systems theory, *see* Walter Buckley, *Sociology and Modern Systems Theory* (Englewood Cliffs, N.J.: Prentice-Hall, 1967), pp. 55–70; and Gordon Hearn, ed., *The General Systems Approach* (New York: Council on Social Work Education, 1969).

6

teristic way of helping clients with difficulties in social functioning and relationships so as to help resolve identity crises and social conflicts and to enable individuals and groups to achieve self-realization and development. Perlman has helped revitalize this orientation in her discussions of persona and identity.[25]

The therapeutic or *action-change process* is also understood in different terms. Such elements as skills, resources, and relationship are applied in a plan or program of action in which services and procedures are combined to realize specific tasks and goals. A basic element of treatment is a shared diagnostic experience between worker and client in which redefinitions of the client's situation and problems take place and mutual problem-solving plans are formulated. The task program is then carried out through the use of one or more strategies involving roles to be performed by the worker, client, and others, as well as specific resources and tactics to be used in some sequential order of process. The social worker's helping interventions are more than "techniques"; they are change-inducing units of behavior and are essentially interactional role performances responsive to heuristic task requirements. .

Situational interventions are concerned with changing relationship and functioning patterns in a group and with altering the group's focus of attention and effort, its definition of experience, and its time-space characteristics. The family and extended family thus become a client, and intake is understood to involve inducting the family unit into the role of client. Change programs are geared to influence organizational and community networks. Marital, family, and milieu therapies as well as family life education programs are again reestablished as basic social work services. The provision of a situational support and reinforcement system for new behavior and interpersonal

relationship patterns is of critical importance in the rehabilitation and resocialization programs of social treatment. For example, in order for a woman to become a more effective mother, she may have to be helped to gain a new understanding of herself and resolve a negative self-image and transference reaction that confirm her to be rejecting and inadequate. In addition her home situation may be transformed into a learning experience. The mother, father, and child, individually and as a family unit, may be guided in learning new attitudes, self-expectations, and role performance skills. Also, family and neighborhood situations may be changed to create a positive environment that is socially reinforcing of more adaptive behavior and relationships.

PROBLEM-TASK FOCUS

Another aspect of the method of social treatment is its *problem-task focus*. The problems of social work clients can be understood as difficulties in completing crucial life tasks, especially the developmental tasks of identity formation and change and transition to new social roles and relationships that occur during the crises of life cycles and careers. Studt describes "task focus" as situational diagnosis and planning, an emphasis on interventive strategies, and a process of establishing and guiding task-oriented working relationships that center around the therapeutic organizational role of the client.[26] The social worker thus becomes a "strategy guide," implementing various kinds of resocializing strategies, with method being adapted creatively to task needs.

A problem-task focus operationally involves identifying and translating a problem into a task or set of tasks to be completed that will overcome obstacles, relieve

---

[25] Helen Harris Perlman, *Persona* (Chicago: University of Chicago Press, 1968).

[26] Elliot Studt, "Social Work Theory and Implications for the Practice of Methods," *Social Work Education Reporter*, Vol. 16, No. 2 (June 1968), pp. 22–24 and 42–46.

7

stress, and achieve desired and specific goals. The accomplishment of such tasks calls for certain essential elements—problem-solving attitudes, motivation, knowledge and skills, resources, consensual goals and strategies, and focused energy (elbow grease)—to be contributed by the client, social worker, social welfare aides, relatives, and other persons who may be available. Thus a depressive reaction on the part of a wife may be redefined as secondary to a marital conflict. Helping efforts would aim to resolve the conflicted role expectations and role performance difficulties between husband and wife, children, and in-laws, and would aim to help the couple learn the competencies needed for a satisfying marriage.

The problem-task orientation places responsibility on the client for conscious participation in decisions regarding goals, risks, costs, and resources to be used in achieving results. Rather than assuming the role of a dependent patient, the client becomes responsible for himself and the social worker acts as a task collaborator. This is a more democratic and efficient division of labor. The organizational role and treatment career of the client offer arrangements through which he can change deviant and discredited identities and learn new values and skills.[27]

The multiple, complicated, severe, and chronic problems often presented by clients also require many different kinds of helping persons—what Studt calls a "work group." [28] Such a helping system may consist of the social worker and client, his relatives and work colleagues, other social workers and helping professionals, as well as social work aides. The social worker often serves as a central member and "clinical team leader." Tasks, rather than cases, may be referred when necessary to obtain external resources or expertise. There is much less dependence on psychiatric consultation or supervision. A premium is placed on role variety, the phasing and coordination of task effort, and team cohesion and morale.

Task structure becomes an important determinant of change strategies and roles as well as of group leadership. The structural elements may be identified, according to Fiedler, in terms of "decision verifiability," "goal clarity," "goal path multiplicity," and "solution specificity," so that tasks can be programmed in step-by-step fashion.[29] Fiedler also suggests certain characteristics of a task: the degree of the task's structure and stress, the interlocking of effort by group members, and the degree of chance or skill perceived as being involved in its completion. The effectiveness of group leadership in utilizing task-oriented or relationship-oriented styles and the productivity of the group are therefore determined by the task structure, the type of group involved, the nature of leader-member relationships, and the position and power of the leader.

One implication of these ideas about task focus and group leadership is that the group leadership role may alternate among worker, client, and others, depending on task needs. Also, it becomes a basic therapeutic objective to improve the leadership competence of the family and group members and the group's problem-solving skills. In addition the natural, unofficial helping system of mutual aid available to an individual and family needs to be strengthened to help them meet recurrent crises of the life cycle. Then the social worker can phase himself out of the client group and terminate treatment.

---

[27] Max Siporin, "Deviant Behavior Theory in Social Work: Diagnosis and Treatment," *Social Work* Vol. 10, No. 3 (July 1965), pp. 59–67.

[28] Studt, op. cit.; and Studt, "Fields of Social Work Practice," *Social Work*, Vol. 10, No. 4 (October 1965), pp. 156–165.

[29] Fred E. Fiedler, *A Theory of Leadership Effectiveness* (New York: McGraw-Hill Book Co., 1967), pp. 22–35 and 142–147.

TABLE 1. ROLE INTERVENTION MODEL FOR PERSONALITY AND SOCIAL SYSTEMS

System Function	Purpose and Outcome	Helping Process	Helping Roles
Pattern maintenance	Identity confirmation	Therapy and identity change	Therapist, healer, consoler, nurturer, confirmer, supporter
Integration	Inclusion, adjustment, unity	Friendship and communion	Friend, social parent, Big Brother, protector, custodian, controller
Adaptation	Growth and competence	Education and socialization	Teacher, guide, model, norm-sender, demonstrator
Goal attainment	Productivity, creativity, self-realization	Problem-solving and task performance	Counselor, expert, adviser, advocate, troubleshooter, mediator, resource person, expediter, referrer

ROLE INTERVENTION

Today the social worker is more helpful in group leadership and membership roles rather than limiting himself to being a confidante or "guru" in intimate encounters with individual clients. He needs to know and be skilled in both individual and group helping procedures and know how to be a group discussion leader. The helping stance is an activist one; he must be direct, self-assertive, and influential so that he can intervene and set in motion change processes that can alter severely pathological interaction patterns, particularly in family crisis situations. The activist, interventive posture has been well described in the case of the worker as family group therapist, but it needs to be extended to other helping situations.[30] Such an orientation encourages a more positive, autonomous kind of self-image for the worker, is self-confirming, and encourages him to be more responsible and accountable for his practice.

The social worker also needs to learn to make a more conscious, direct, and therapeutic use of his authority so that he can alter power structures and communication patterns in a disorganized family, terminate vicious self-reinforcing habitual cycles of sadomasochistic relationships, or obtain scarce community resources. Not only in protective cases involving abused or neglected children, but in many other kinds of situations as well, therapeutic tasks demand a firm, limited, and directive influence based on important professional and personal forms of authority as well as on agency-delegated bureaucratic authority. The client views a therapeutic use of authority as real, powerful influence on his behalf. Such exercise of authority needs to be consistent with democratic ethics and forms—allowing freedom and choice for the client—within the collaborative contract and relationship between client and worker.

As a representative of the social work profession, the social worker takes on a

[30] Arthur L. Leader, "The Role of Intervention in Family Group Treatment," *Social Casework*, Vol. 45, No. 6 (June 1964), pp. 327–332; and Virginia Satir, *Conjoint Family Therapy* (Palo Alto, Calif.: Science and Behavior Books, 1967).

9

multifunctional orientation as he seeks to help realize the profession's institutional and societal tasks. He does this by using helping processes that are problem solving, educational, therapeutic, and socially integrative. These processes articulate with the functional prerequisites of personality and social systems identified by Parsons as system "pattern variables" of pattern maintenance, integration, adaptation, and goal attainment.[31] The helping processes are also linked to outcomes of identity confirmation, social inclusion and adjustment, growth and competence, and productivity and self-realization for individuals and collectivities. In turn the helping processes are fulfilled through a wide repertoire of helping roles. These multidimensional relationships are listed in Table 1.

In social treatment the social worker serves as a system change agent for both personality and social systems. He seeks to be active and effective at several levels of intervention, choosing targets and entry points in individual, family, group, organizational, community, and institutional structures and domains of functioning. Geismar, Spergel, and others have illustrated this multilevel approach in the provision of individualized services.[32] There is, however, a growing awareness that it is through his role performances in situational interventions that the social worker gains entry and effects change for personality and social systems, including the social welfare system.

Role performances are extremely important in carrying out helping interventions. A social system consists of patterns of role relationships actualized by people in social situations. Meaningful action is role-patterned behavior oriented toward symbolic or overt situational interaction with others. One has to be a role-actor to participate socially and function as a human being. Role performances thus are ways of getting jobs done and of meeting reciprocal needs for identity and reality confirmation. They also dramatize and idealize a social situation so as to maximize one's influence on the behavior of others.[33] Therefore, it is through his role performances that the social worker acts in reciprocal and collaborative relationships with clients and carries out the jobs of giving information, changing attitudes and behavior, motivating, limiting, modeling, and so forth.

In order to have maximum therapeutic influence, the social worker needs to provide effective role performances in which he is genuine and committed. The roles may be culturally defined and should be geared to the client's expectations. But they will be interpreted personally by each worker and enacted in highly individualistic styles. Even when they are part of the social rituals of degradation or conversion ceremonies, the social worker may have to improvise the helping roles in response to the often unpredictable contingencies of situational events and the often unpredictable behavior of clients and others.

In social treatment processes, the social worker is active either within or outside a social agency office and intervenes directly or indirectly in the client's life situations. He accomplishes his therapeutic tasks through an extensive repertoire of general

[31] Talcott Parsons, "Pattern Variables Revisited," *American Sociological Review*, Vol. 25, No. 4 (August 1960), pp. 467–483. For an effort to relate these Parsonian pattern variables to helping roles in residential treatment, *see* Howard W. Polsky and Daniel S. Claster, "The Structure and Functions of Adult-Youth Systems," in Muzafer Sherif and Carolyn Sherif, eds., *Problems of Youth* (Chicago: Aldine Publishing Co., 1965), pp. 189–211.

[32] Ludwig L. Geismar, "Three Levels of Treatment for the Multiproblem Family," *Social Casework*, Vol. 42, No. 3 (March 1961), pp. 124–127; and Irving Spergel, "A Multi-Dimensional Model for Social Work Practice," *Social Service Review*, Vol. 36, No. 1 (March 1962), pp. 62–71.

[33] Erving Goffman, *The Presentation of Self in Everyday Life* (New York: Doubleday Anchor Books, 1969), pp. 17–76.

and specific situational roles.[34] The most highly valued role—therapist—is now often overshadowed by other diverse roles such as integrator and friend, problem-solving expert and innovator, mediator and negotiator, liaison person and coordinator of resources (broker), spokesman (advocate), and especially teacher.

The therapeutic work of consoling, nurturing, and confirming the self-worth and identity of a client needs to be done in conjunction with helping actions of the friend and social parent. The resolution of intrapsychic and interpersonal conflicts and the integration of new identities and social roles as well as the integration of individuals within collectivities are now seen as reciprocal aspects of a social inclusion process carried out with peers and parental surrogates.

The social worker is, as always, expected to be an expert troubleshooter who can intervene in severe crises, mediate violent disputes, negotiate and find innovative resolutions for impossible difficulties. But high value is accorded the provider and coordinator of social supports and community resources needed for the client's development and problem-solving adaptation. As resource person and procedural guide the worker actively uses intergroup community processes within the unofficial, natural helping system of the client's social network. Or he deals directly with the official social welfare community and bureaucracies to make available to the client varied social provisions and social utilities such as financial aid, day care, and homemaker and medical care services. The spokesman (advocate) role is one that does not relieve social workers of their obligations to the community and the social welfare institution they represent, but it does call for them to give priority again to the needs and interests of the clients and citizens the welfare community is intended to serve. It also demands that social workers be identified again as social reformers, encouraging changes in values and client participation in social action programs that have both therapeutic and social betterment objectives.

It is as a therapeutic teacher, guiding individual and group learning processes, that the social worker is meeting crucial needs in our society. The current conflicts and dislocations of the urban scene are in part due to processes of vast social migration and mobility; they require extensive social reforms and individualized resocialization-educational programs. Thus social workers help clients acquire the cognitive development, social competence, and the social adjustment or role satisfaction that is also called mental health. They teach clients the skills of deriving maximum benefits from the social security and welfare bureaucratic systems, about which knowledge and skill have become essential for socialization and rehabilitation programs.[35] Still further, they enable the client to learn meaningful personal and social philosophies, live by valid values and standards, and gain viable identities as individual and family members in human communities.

In these therapeutic, integrative, educational, and problem-solving processes, the dynamics of change depend heavily on potent group and situational forces.[36] These influences facilitate the emergence of creative individual and collective adjustment efforts and what Durkheim called a "collective consciousness." In social treatment programs, the social worker can direct

[34] For a definition and discussion of situational roles, see Max Siporin, "Private Practice of Social Work: Functional Roles and Social Control," Social Work, Vol. 6, No. 2 (April 1961), pp. 52–60.

[35] Otto Pollak identifies these kinds of skills in "The Outlook for the American Family," Journal of Marriage and the Family, Vol. 29, No. 1 (February 1967), pp. 193–205.

[36] These situational change forces are well discussed by Alan F. Klein, "Individual Change Through Group Experience," National Conference on Social Welfare, 1959 (New York: Columbia University Press, 1959), pp. 136–155.

his role performances so that they are complementary and reinforcing for new and adaptive role identities and performances on the part of the client and other members of his natural groups. Expectations and mutual aid efforts that operate to effect behavioral and situational changes are activated.

Operationally this means that the social worker does not play Big Daddy to the Baby Boy or rescuer of the sinner, but he does encourage adult, friendly, altruistic relationships and corrective therapeutic experiences. He fosters dyadic and team task performances that move to accomplish concrete tasks and reward effort, learning, self-disclosure, and authenticity for the client and significant others. He enables the collective "interexperience," characterized by a common consciousness of meanings, values, and relationships and a mutual commitment to them.[37] It is through such an interexperience that problems get resolved and support is given to interdependence and individuality, to a sense of personal and social responsibility as well as to the inherent processes of individual and social growth.

SUMMARY AND CONCLUSIONS

Social treatment is a new-old mode of helping individuals and family groups. Social workers feel comfortable with it because of its old associations yet excited by the new aspects and rich potential for more relevant and effective service to clients.

In current practice social treatment is distinguished by patterns of service that may be said to constitute a new helping method. It is based on a traditional problem-person-situation model for diagnosis and interventive change (also found to be a systems model), for which a variety of theories are useful in an eclectic fashion.

Assessment and treatment processes have new aspects in this approach, with a problem-task focus that has important consequences for a more democratic, collaborative relationship between client and worker. There is a renewed emphasis on social situational helping interventions and group leadership by the social worker through role performances that are activist, multifunctional, versatile, and directed toward the accomplishment of both personality and social system change. Situational interventions can use potent social interactional forces and enable the emergence of a collective consciousness and adaptive experience through which adjustment problems are resolved and individual and group growth are nourished.

Further development of the theory, principles, and procedures of social treatment need direct attention. There is need to determine, for example, how different kinds of problems shape different patterns of services and how differential tasks affect the choice of helping strategies and roles for client and social worker. There is also need to clarify the effectiveness of social treatment programs for specific change in individual behavior and social relationships. Hopefully research about social treatment will again provide, as it did in the past, the hard data about poverty, illness, pathology, and social conditions to support programs of social legislation.

The method of social treatment and the changes in practice associated with it have already stimulated much-needed change in social work education. The delivery of programmatic services and the social work manpower needed for such delivery systems have made for a vast increase in the training of different levels of personnel and for a renewed emphasis on preparation for administrative, program-planning, and evaluative functions. Because it is here that we have allowed unhelpful gaps and vacuums in leadership and service, there is also need to give greater priority to the training of doctorate-level practitioners for frontline

---

[37] The concept and process of interexperience are presented by R. D. Laing, *The Politics of Experience* (New York: Pantheon, 1967), p. 19.

12

service functions and team-leadership roles.

Social treatment appears eminently suitable for the needed structure of direct individualized social work services that can effect behavioral and situational change for clients. As developed during the earlier and the current social reform eras, social treatment gives prominence to the social purposes of the profession and helps social workers recapture the earlier utopian, yet pragmatic, social vision needed today. Hopefully social workers may now be better able to halt the extreme oscillations and establish the balance between the individual rehabilitation and social reform orientations that Mary Richmond and Porter Lee wished for and that have yet to be achieved. With this new-old method of social treatment, social workers can better respond to today's social crises and aid people to achieve both the individual identity and community they so greatly desire.

13

CAO–004–C

BY DAVID WINEMAN

The Life-Space Interview

THE PRESENT ARTICLE describes an interview approach—the life-space interview—originated by Fritz Redl under specific conditions of practice with ego-disturbed children—and contrasts it with traditional interview techniques found in clinical social work practice.

The greatest single influence on the interview method in clinical social work has come, of course, from classical psychoanalytic treatment practice. *Content* most eagerly sought by the classical therapist is that which refers to the libidinal relationship to the parents and siblings of the client, on both conscious and unconscious levels. Interview *relationship and role structure* are most carefully guarded against contamination from either the therapist's or client's ongoing life experiences; neither the therapist nor the client may have such ties with each other as could involve either or both with the opportunity for gratification of the other or direct power over each other's behavior away from the interview setting. Finally, the *time-space conditions* under which all clinical events take place are strictly defined in an appointment hour (time) and in the therapist's office (space).

The original psychoanalytic model from which this is borrowed is best suited, and was originally developed clinically, for the classical adult neurotic. Although complexly disturbed, he sacrifices the least of his ego to his illness, as compared with other disturbance syndromes, and his principal *ego strain* is experienced in connection with his specific conflicts, leaving him free to cope with most other adjustive tasks in a normal way. However, when we come to the child neurotic, things are a little different—even with the "classical" child neurotic. Redl [1] reminds us that Anna Freud herself explicitly recognized that certain modifications of adult therapy techniques were necessary because of the incompleteness in ego development and the nature of the child's relationship to the adult world. These modifications raised the ceiling on how far the therapist could directly invade libidinal, reality, and value spheres, as compared with adult therapy. Thus, one of Miss Freud's girl patients was seriously advised by her that while it was

DAVID WINEMAN, M.S.W., *is associate professor of social work at Wayne State University, Detroit, Michigan.*

[1] Fritz Redl, "Strategy and Techniques of the Life-Space Interview," *American Journal of Orthopsychiatry,* Vol. 28, No. 1 (January 1959).

Reprinted from SOCIAL WORK, 4 (January 1959), pp 3–17. Copyright © by the National Association of Social Workers, Inc., 1959.

CAO–005–C

perfectly all right to use obscene language in telling her fantasies to Miss Freud, this was "out" anywhere else. Specific directions and suggestions of a management or training type could be made to parents. On the gratification level, candy bars, soft drinks, and cookies are far from infrequent in orthodox therapy with children of less than pubertal age.

Yet, in spite of these shifts toward more involvement in the libidinal, reality, or value zones of the child's life, classical child therapy—casework or psychoanalytic—sticks with *content* focus on libidinal materials of a historically determined type, becomes involved in ongoing reality areas only to "save" the therapy from oblivion, and, while permitting gratifications to the child, holds these down to the bare minimum required to involve the child in a relationship. Also the classical *space-time* condition of the office appointment is preserved.

So much for a brief structural analysis of the "classical" interview concept and its modifications for work with children. Now let us examine the origin and development of the "life-space" concept which in some ways only carries further the modifications begun by Anna Freud, and in others is clearly different along qualitative lines.

LIFE-SPACE CONCEPT

In the early 1940's, Fritz Redl was operating both summer camp and winter club groups in the city for severely ego-disturbed children, who had been referred by various Detroit social agencies with whom the children were simultaneously in individual therapy. As experience accumulated in these projects, it was noticed that frequently a child might produce behavior (temper tantrums, swiftly appearing sulks and withdrawals, stealing, fighting) that required on-the-spot handling of an interview-like type, the responsibility for which was assumed by the adult in charge, usually a group worker or a group work–field work student. Upon analysis, the types of interviews [2] that grew out of this proved to hold a technical complexity and meaning that any good casework or psychiatric interview might have, even though the locus of interview was much more a part of the *life-space* of the child, its content released by a piece of unplanned *life-space* dynamics and was being performed by an *"out-of-role" person who had direct life-experiential meaning for the child on reality, value, and libidinal terms.* Thus, while the classical approach would specify that reality issues should be handled only when they endanger therapy, the life-space approach would insist that with severely ego-damaged children they provide some necessary materials without which therapy could not go on. Yet—and this is important—it does not argue that traditional methods cannot also be of powerful assistance and readily concedes that both methods can be applied in the service of therapy with the same child. Thus, for instance, many of the episodes that were the target of life-space interviewing in the club groups were also picked up by the agency therapist later on, either being brought in by the child himself or raised by the worker who was always in communication with the project leader.

Beginning in this way, the life-space approach was further experimented with at Pioneer House (1946–48),[3] a residential treatment home for boys, at the children's ward and residence at National Institute of Mental Health in Bethesda (1953–present),[4]

[2] Redl first used the term "marginal" instead of "life space" for these interviews. The reasons for this shift are interesting but not crucial to this paper. One reason, as Redl wryly puts it: "The term marginal lost the clarity of its meaning besides the low-status meaning the term 'marginal' seems to hold for some people."

[3] Fritz Redl and David Wineman, *Controls from Within* (Glencoe, Ill.: The Free Press, 1951).

[4] Fritz Redl, "Strategy and Techniques of the Life Space Interview," *op. cit.*

Joel Vernick, "Illustrations of Strategy Problems in Life Space Interviewing Around Situations of Behavioral Crises," paper presented at the 1957 Annual

2

and at the University of Michigan Fresh Air Camp, a summer camp for disturbed boys (1950–present) [5] from which setting the clinical material for the present paper is drawn.

GOALS, TASKS, AND LEVELS OF FUNCTION

The type of child around whose treatment life-space interviewing has been developed finds it virtually impossible to manage himself for a single day without the eruption of behavioral episodes representing in one way or another his disturbances in ego functioning. In this section we shall try to examine the ways in which these episodes may be used by the clinician as potential content for life-space interviewing, and the kinds of goals, tasks, and levels of function that have been tentatively worked out for this style of interview. As an opening illustration, let us take a look at Ricki,[6] one of our last season's Fresh Air campers in one of his "bad" moments.

Ricki, an 11-year-old boy with a chain-style history of broken foster home placements, was a terribly deprived, bitter child with an insatiable, violent hunger for proofs of affection from the adult and an equally intense expectation of treachery and deceit. Imagine, then, his reaction when one day, after an acrimonious dispute between himself and another camper over the ownership of a

Meeting of the American Orthopsychiatric Association.

Allen T. Dittmann and Howard L. Kitchener, "Life Space Interviewing and Individual Play Therapy: A Comparison of Techniques," *American Journal of Orthopsychiatry*, Vol. 29, No. 1 (January 1959).

William C. Morse and Edna R. Small, "Group Life Space Interviewing in a Therapeutic Camp," *American Journal of Orthopsychiatry*, Vol. 29, No. 1 (January 1959).

[5] William Morse and David Wineman, "Group Interviewing in a Camp for Disturbed Boys," *The Journal of Social Issues*, Vol. 13, No. 1 (1957). Also, for the interested, this issue carries several articles on the University of Michigan camp and its operation.

[6] All campers' names are pseudonyms.

walking cane which had been made in the camp craft shop, the facts supported the other child and we had to take the cane from Ricki and give it to the other youngster. He blew up immediately, had to be physically prevented from slugging the other boy, accused us of being in league with the other boy, and so on.

At the point of eruption of this "symptomatic" behavior, the adult on the scene will have to decide in which of two basic directions Ricki's interview handling should go:

1. He may simply try to "pull him through" the behavioral storm and sit it out with him until he is controlled enough to go about his regular business of life at camp. In addition to this protective waiting it out with him, we would also try to take the edge off his suspicion about our being in "cahoots" with the other boy by going over the facts again of how the mixup in the craft shop had occurred so that the other boy's cane had been mistakenly given to Ricki. And we would display our eagerness for him to have a cane by offering immediately to detail a staff member to help him start a new one, thus alleviating his frustration in having to wait until the next morning when the craft shop would be open again.

2. Our on-the-scene adult, instead of merely sitting it out with Ricki and getting him started on a new walking cane, might see this as a good opportunity to pick up this particular blow-up (which was a repetition of many that Ricki had already had) as a typical instance of his "problem," point out that this was the way he reacted *whenever* things didn't go the way he wanted them to, that we knew that even back in the foster homes he had these blow-ups, and so on. In other words, in Step 2 the adult tries to use this situation toward the realization of a long-range clinical "improvement goal." (Actually in this case we went only as far as Step 1 because Ricki was still too confused about himself and his problems to have enough "uninfected ego" on tap for

3

use in picking up a useful perception of any part of the self in relation to a long-range goal.)

Redl has given these two major uses of the life-space interview characteristically descriptive titles.[7] Simply pulling a child through a tough spot (our Step 1) he calls "emotional first aid on the spot." If, in addition, the incident is tactically aimed at the long-range goal (our Step 2) he calls it "clinical exploitation of life events." However, the dichotomy is anything but a tight one. Not infrequently, there may be a coupling of the two functions or a switch midstream in the interview. Following the dichotomy with this warning in mind, let us now examine some of the subfunctions of these two basic functions.

CLINICAL EXPLOITATION OF LIFE EVENTS

Clinical "exploitation"[8] is a broad term. A clinical goal, upon inspection, becomes a network of subgoals or tasks which therapy is trying to achieve. Interviews along the way serve now one, now another, of these subgoals. In the category under discussion, the following separate subheadings are aimed at demonstrating this discreteness of function in the life-space interview.

1. REALITY "RUB-IN"

Many ego-damaged children are perceptually confused as to what goes on around them either because they have already woven together a "delusional"[9] system of

life interpretation or because they suffer from a peculiar "drag" of a structural type in their ego development. In either case, many times they don't seem to "get the hang" of a social interaction web unless one puts it together for them with the special magnification aids of the "on-the-spot" style of interview.

Hank, 8½, is removed from his cabin at bedtime in screaming, hitting rage, having already socked his counselor twice in the side. "She didn't have no right to flip me on the floor," he yells, as we take him to the main lodge of the camp, giving in this way his rationale for hitting her. In the lodge, he sits broodingly in a thirty-minute sulk before he will say anything at all, while the counselor and I sit with him, the latter having been relieved by another staff member so she can stay with Hank and me. As his rage drains out and in response to our encouragement, he blurts out again, "She didn't have to flip me to the floor!" Then commenced a four-way interview between Hank, Lorie (the counselor), myself, and Dr. Albert Cohen, the camp sociologist.[10]

Lorie: *(replying to Hank's statement that she "flipped" him)* This is not the way it really happened, Hank. Remember you've been jumping on me, poking me, and pulling on me most of the afternoon and evening.

Hank: *(somewhat defiantly but smiling a little)* Aw, that was just in fun. You didn't even care about *that.*

Lorie: I asked you to stop many times.

Hank: Well, yeah, but you really didn't care though.

Cohen: Hank, let's talk about what happened in the cabin tonight. Here was Lorie trying to get you guys to bed—right?

Hank: Right.

---

[7] Fritz Redl, "Strategy and Techniques of the Life Space Interview," *op. cit.*

[8] Throughout this article I am following the nomenclature of the life-space interview and its major as well as subfunctions originated by Redl and appearing in his article "Strategy and Techniques of the Life-Space Interview," *op. cit.*, and also, in part, in our joint volume, *Controls from Within, op. cit.*

[9] The term "delusional" is used to connote a kind of persistent, perceptual distortion of a somewhat persecutory type which is frequently found in impulse-disordered children. Since, however, many of them have really been badly handled by the adult world, this is not classically paranoid. Yet in treat-

ing the "good" adult as though he were the same as the "bad," they commit a delusional error.

[10] All examples are drawn from the University of Michigan Fresh Air Camp experience of 1958. In each instance the writer was the interviewer except where otherwise specified. Each interview sample is the product of postinterview "selective" recall. Both individual and group interviews are included and will be identified as such.

4

Cohen: And what were you doing?

Hank: I was holdin' on to her.

Cohen: How?

Hank: I was grabbin' her around the middle from behind. I had my arms around hers (*pinning her arms*).

Cohen: And Lorie is busy trying to help the other guys get ready for bed.

Hank: Yeah.

Cohen: And the other guys may need things that she has to get or want her to do some things for them, too.

Hank: Yeah.

Cohen: Lorie is tired and she's been asking you to quit jumping on her most of the afternoon and evening but you're still grabbing her and won't let her go.

Hank: Guess so—but she didn't have to flip me.

Cohen: Did she *ask* you to let her go?

Hank: Yeah.

Cohen: How many times?

Hank: Three or four.

Cohen: So she *asks* you to let go. But you keep hanging on to her. Now, (*gently and emphatically*) she's asked you many times but you still hang on. She wants you to let go because she is tired of all the jumping and hanging on and has all these things to do which she can't because you're dragging on her. What do you think she should do?

Hank: Dunno.

Cohen: She has to get loose, doesn't she?

Hank: Guess so.

Cohen: So she spreads her arms forcing you to let go—right?

Hank: Yes.

Cohen: Could she have done it any other way?

Hank: (*without anger and quite readily*) No—guess not.

Wineman: Then you fell to the cabin floor?

Hank: Yeah.

Wineman: Then what happened?

Hank: The kids laughed and I got mad.

Wineman: I guess we can all see that that would be hard to take. And then?

Hank: I socked Lorie.

Wineman: Hank, right after you socked Lorie, how did you expect she felt toward you?

Hank: Sore at me.

Wineman: And because you thought she was sore at you, what else did you think about her and you?

Hank: That she wouldn't like me.

Wineman: And then?

Hank: I got mad all over again.

Wineman: And then?

Hank: I socked her again.

Wineman: That's about when I came into the cabin, isn't it? (*He nods.*) And she was havin' to hold you because you were so sore. Then I took you over here and at first you were still so sore you wouldn't talk or anything and still kept thinking that she had tried to flip you on purpose—right?

Hank: Yeah. (*By now he is smiling rather brightly; his mood has changed from sullen and defiant to cheerful agreement; actually he seems to enjoy the careful empathic unraveling of the episode.*)

At this point, it seems that Hank has a much clearer perception of his own role in the production of the cabin situation and the "flip" by Lorie. At first he sees her as an aggravator and rejector, blots out entirely his own persistent, somewhat erotic, pestering of her and his blocking of her carrying out of her duties in the cabin in relation to the whole group. This series of perceptions is the target of the first part of the interview. Next he sees that the group reaction to his unfortunate fall "burns him up" and grasps the relation between this and slugging the counselor the first time. Finally, he understands that once he has "socked her" he expects retaliation from her in the form of rejection (Note: He does not expect to get "socked" in return, showing his basically *correct* understanding of our policy against physical punishment). This, he sees, makes him even more angry *so he hits her again.* Then comes the finale in the lodge.

In terms of *goal,* this type of interview is both short-range and long-range in its intent: short-range, we want to help Hank stop mauling the counselor *as soon as possible.* Long-range, through the "injection"

CAO—005—C

of many such interview episodes, we want him (1) to become more habituated and skilled in self-observation and (2) to step up his sensitivity to the feelings and emotions of people upon whom he is acting in an interpersonal chain. Hank's postinterview behavior in relation to this single item —mauling the counselor—improved, by the way, so that the short-range goal can be said to have been achieved. Obviously, as stated, only multiple exposure can attack the long-range problem but this may be seen as a link along the way.

2. SYMPTOM ESTRANGEMENT

Another characteristic of the children in connection with whose treatment the life-space interview has been developed is that instead of finding any part of their functioning strange or bothersome (as does the conventional "treatment-prone" neurotic) they have invested heavily in secondary gain ventures to such an extent that the whole ego seems to be allied with their central pathology rather than any part of the ego taking a stand against it. While this does not mean that the whole ego is sick with the same disease that we are trying to cure, unless its "uninfected" part can be "estranged" from the core pathology and converted into an allegiance to seeing that "something is wrong," the clinical battle cannot even get started. The life-space interview has shown itself to be peculiarly fitted for this crucial, initial task.

Don, 10 years old, is so intensely driven toward the image of a teen-age "hood" that he seems to have stepped out of a "cornier-than-life" Hollywood movie of this type of kid. He has been an addict smoker since the age of 6, steals, knows all of the crude sex terms and practices, and lies with the aplomb of an Alcatraz lifer when "caught with the goods." An adopted child of a near-to-middle class family, he has overwhelmed his adoptive father with the force of his "delinquent" identification, spurring the father into alternating fits of brutality and mawkish,

sentimental surrender of a defeatist type. Any admitted perception on Don's part that he is ever scared, might need protection against more powerful kids, or that he might, in any cell of his being, have a "little boy" part seems to have been ruthlessly ground out of awareness. The following episode was one of the first clinical demonstration chances we had at camp to trap his ego into what might be considered a potentially "treatment positive" perception. It all happened as a result of Don's having sadistically teased one of his cabin mates by shaking a tree branch that this boy was perched on, in spite of the other one's terrified screams for Don to stop, and, then later on the same day, ripping up another cabin mate's Sorry cards because the second boy would not give Don a snake he had caught. These two seemingly unrelated events were "stitched" together in the following interview in such a way that Don's fear motivation was made visible to him.

Interviewer: Don, do I have this straight—when Terry was yelling for you to stop shaking the branch, you kept on doing it anyway?
Don: Yep.
Int.: And then what would Terry do?
Don: Keep yellin' for me to stop.
Int.: But the more he yelled the more you what —— ?
Don: Shook 'im.
Int.: Why do you suppose he was yelling?
Don: Because he was scared.
Int.: Yet the more scared he got, the more it seems you felt like shaking him.
Don: That's right.
Int.: I wonder why you'd want to do that—make him scared?
Don: I dunno.
Int.: That'd be something I should think you'd want to know about yourself —don't you agree?
Don: (uneasily) Yeah.
The interview then moves on to the second incident of the same day—tearing up the Sorry cards.
Int.: Don, how come you ripped up Rusty's Sorry cards?

6

Don: (indignantly) Heck—he promised me the next snake he caught and after he caught this here snake he never gave it to me.

Int.: Well, I guess he should've gone through with his deal, although I'm not saying you had the right to tear up his cards because he didn't. Anyway, how come you don't catch your own snakes?

Don: (indignantly again) I'll bet you'd like to get bit by a snake on yer finger?

Int.: No, I wouldn't. You mean you are scared enough of snakes that you try to get Rusty to give you one of his? Not take the risk of catching one yourself?

Don: Yeah, boy.

Int.: And yet when Terry is up in the tree you do everything you can to make him more what ——?

Don: (disgustedly) Scared!

Int.: That's right Don, scared. So now I begin to wonder to myself. Maybe Don wants to make other guys scared because if he can be such a guy as can scare other guys, then he doesn't have to be so what ——?

Don: (spits it out) Scared!

Int.: Yep—that's right again—scared.

Don: (blustering) Yeah—yeah. (in his most "gravelly" voice) Next time my ma comes I'm gonna ask her to bring two of my buddies, they'll tell you I don't get scared.

Int.: Easy, boy, easy! I'm not saying you're chicken or that you get scared all the time. Heck, anybody gets scared about certain things—there's nothing wrong with that. But you—you don't like to admit you get scared hardly at all. Go around actin' like you're a teen-ager, smoking, stealing and all that. You do, don't you? We've been through that before.

Don: Yeah.

Int.: So all I'm sayin' now is that maybe some of that stuff is mixed up with your tryin' to make out that you don't scare easy—see? That's about all I'm saying. And you're already in plenty of trouble back home on account of doin' that, aren't you?

Don: (unhappily) Yeah.

Don, of course, is far from happy with any of this. In fact, he is "burned up." The clinical issue, however, is the question: is he any wiser? We think he may be—a wee, but crucial, bit. Also, it puts us in a much more favorable position to urge Don to take more seriously the camp caseworker's attempts to get at his problem as well as to take a new look at what his worker in the city is trying to do for him. This, followed by continuing interview coverage which explores his fear motivation, is an important step in working back to his whole tough-guy reaction formation against being little and helpless. (Of course, there is a hard possibility that Don cannot be helped by anything short of residential treatment anyway, but that is another story and not for these pages.)

3. VALUE REPAIR AND RESTORATION

The ego-disturbed child handles still another major adjustive task very unskillfully: that of bringing about a proper balance or synthesis between values and behavior. This is a complicated issue and there is not enough space to give it the "phenomenological respect" it deserves. Briefly, with the children under consideration, there are three aspects of this problem:

a. There may be some *deficiencies* in value content: certain pieces of superego have never been formed.

b. There may be some *uniquenesses* in value content: certain pieces of superego are formed but are different, sometimes to the point of opposition, from the value pattern of the dominant, surrounding social environment.

c. Regardless of what value content there may be to begin with, the *superego is incompletely introjected,* still depends in its functioning upon the presence of "adult enforcers," and is feared and fought by the ego.

These three possibilities are not necessarily mutually exclusive; in fact, with the type of children being discussed they are

7

usually interwoven. The resulting clinical challenge involves us in the task of helping them become more sensitive to the demands of whatever superego has already been built into the personality, or rebuilding it or modifying it as the case may be. Since the admission of guilt is often fought off by these children out of fear of peer-group derision or rejection as "adult lovers," it is especially important to reconnoiter their myriad interpersonal squabbles and feuds for "clean" issues where potentially culpable children can be spared this expensive prestige payment in front of their buddies.

A group of 11-year-olds was being seen with the purpose of trying to help them figure out why they were continually at each other's throats, battling, cursing, teasing each other with cruel tricks, and, in general, unmanageable by their counselors. As typically happens, at the outset they all heaped responsibility on a particular youngster who served as chief scapegoat.

Int. (Al Cohen): What are some of the things Larry does that make you guys think he causes all the trouble?

Chorus of voices: Calls us "mother names," [11] spits at us, wakes up early in the morning and yells—stuff like that.

Int.: Tell me about the last time he did that.

Joe: This morning I was sitting on my bunk before flag-raising—and I asked him for one of his comics—so he says: "Yer mammy." [12]

Int.: And what did you do?

Joe: I says, "Yer sister."

Int.: And then?

Joe: He throws a shoe at me.

Int.: And then?

Joe: I climbs up on his bunk and slugs him—that's what!

Chuck: (a third boy) Yeah, and he always does stuff like that. That's how we get in trouble.

Int.: Who else had fights today?

Sam: (a fourth boy) I did—with Chuck!

Int.: How come?

Sam: Aw, we come out of the swim and he calls my mother a name.

Int.: Chuck, is that right?

Chuck: Yeah—'cause that bastard [Sam] flicked his towel at me!

Sam: The hell I did—I just threw it over my shoulder!

Bill: (a fifth boy) 'n this so-an-so (pointing at Jim, a sixth member of the group) flicks his towel at me.

Int.: What was Larry doing all this time?

Group: (Silence)

Int.: You mean he wasn't involved at all?

Voices: Naw!

Int.: Look. First you guys start off by saying that Larry starts all the trouble, but here are Joe, Chuck, Bill, Sam, and Jim all at each other, yelling mother names, slugging with towels, spitting—and Larry wasn't in on it at all. He sure couldn't have started this one, could he? I wonder how fair it is to accuse him of starting "everything."

Group: (Amazed silence, then agreement.)

Joe: (his principal accuser) Boy, it sure wouldn't be easy to be him!

It is clear that this quite amazing pinpointing of a piece of group unfairness could hardly have emerged so cleanly without a close "life-space probe" resulting in clarification of the behavior chain involved in this particular incident. That the original goal of the interview (to help them achieve some insight into their mutual goading of each other) was only lightly covered detracts hardly at all from the unexpected value lesson so deftly pulled out of the interview by the interviewer. In fact, it hit at one of the contributing factors to the group control problem which was one of tax-exempt shifting away of blame from the self on to the scapegoat. This evasion became much harder for them after such a clear admission of unfairness. The reader may be reminded by this spontaneous inter-

---

[11] A complicated form of verbal teasing by accusing each others' mothers of obscene sex practices.

[12] The unspoken, but understood ending to this expletive is "Yer mammy is a *whore*."

view development of an earlier comment (see page 5) about the difficulty of deciding ahead of time as to exactly which goal a given life-space interview is to be focused upon.

4. NEW TOOL SALESMANSHIP

In this very aptly named subfunction of the life-space interview, Redl has emphasized that one of the severe hazards faced by the ego-disturbed child is linked to the marked impoverishment of his reaction techniques. An important clinical goal, then, is defined by this particle of his pathology: situations must be salvaged from his ongoing experience which can be used to give him a vista of "new tools" that may be applied in moments of problem-solving breakdown.

Chick, a delinquent boy of 9½, who had been booked by the police many times in his short life for larceny and armed robbery—among lighter offenses such as truancy—was a very assaultive child. Early in the camp season, we faced a critical problem in his tendency to slug his female counselors on what appeared to be light provocation. Detailed exploration of these encounters proved that the attacks upon the counselors took place when sudden floods of rage and fear confronted the ego based upon Chick's anticipation of rejection or physical attack from the counselors whom he really liked very much. This seemed to be a severe transference style reaction stemming from a lifetime of exposure to violence and fear at home. However, complex though it was, the transference reaction was not the immediate problem but rather that when Chick was in a fear state, reality-justified or not, the only think he seemed to be able to do was to use his fists or a nearby weapon. Thus, the first problem we attacked was not the reality distortion of his counselors' feelings and motives toward him, but his need to use his fists to begin with whenever he had such feelings. Partly he was *aware* that he was caught in a web of confusion to begin

with, which fact he conveyed to us directly once after we had said, "Chick, you know the counselors aren't like *that*" (meaning that the counselors neither wanted to hurt nor reject him). To which he replied, "Yeah, but sometimes you just *can't believe it*." Our tack with him then became: "Chick, whenever you have those kinds of feelings, use *this (smiling and lightly putting a finger on his mouth)* instead of *these (touching his fists)*. He gave his "crooked" smile and seemed to understand.

Of course this had to be repeated many times—it was not easy to wean Chick from using his fists. Ironically enough, the very next incident, after the above attempt to sell him "word tools" in exchange for slugging, involved his being brought in for *biting* the counselor and then claiming he was using his mouth instead of his fists as he had been asked to! But gradually, and ultimately with pride, he substituted crude verbal statements of fear and rage for action demonstrations as far as the adult was concerned at least.

5. MANIPULATION OF THE BOUNDARIES OF THE SELF

One of the job achievements that proper ego development assures to the individual is that of helping him to learn effectively where he "ends" and other people and/or their rights, privileges, and processes "begin." This is one sector of the larger process of distinction between the self and the non-self that developmental theory posits as one of the major critical achievements of ego growth. Unclear and complex as this process is, it is a certain fact that it is blocked and hamstrung in the type of children under discussion. Thus, in addition to having a core pathology of severe, uncheckable impulsivity, they seem to have much more than a peripheral, additional problem in dealing with other people and situations with the proper degree of auton-

9

omy and self-determination. Breakdown of this ego subfunction results in two widely opposite responses: (a) either other people's excitement quickly becomes theirs, other kids' mischief or aggression quickly racing toward them and covering them as a leaping flame with a gasoline-soaked rag; or (b) quite the reverse, their own feeling tone, whim, or prejudice is narcissistically, sometimes even megalomaniacally, forced upon another individual with no apparent awareness of or concern about the boundary between the own self and the other person, his rights, privileges, and so on.

In other words, in the first reaction, (a), the ego permits itself to be invaded by a "foreign" ego and then functions as though the motivational trend of the invading ego were its own. In the second reaction, (b), the ego invades a "foreign" ego and then functions as though it were the motivational trend of the invaded ego. The pathology is the same, the direction reversed, just as having the delusion that one is dead or is the last person on earth who is living are examples of the same pathology.

An interesting example of the second reaction, as well as a beginning attempt at influencing it, may be found in the following fragment of a long interview with Slim, a violent, but verbal and intelligent 13-year-old. It so happened that Slim intensely disliked a peculiar trait of one of his cabin mates: a habit of walking on his toes whenever he was barefoot.

Slim: He *(other boy)* always stands and walks on his tiptoes. I don't like that. I don't know why but it seems to be just one more reason for not liking him. So I decided, and I told him, that every time I caught him doing that I would snap him with my towel. I'm trying to break him of the habit.

Int.: Do you really feel you have the right to inflict pain upon him just because you don't like it.

Slim: Yeah *(slowly and deliberately).* I really think I do.

Int.: You mean your conscience goes along with this?

Slim: No, it doesn't. I know it's wrong to do but sometimes when I don't like something I feel I have the right to attack it.

Int.: Even though you know it isn't right according to your conscience.

Slim: My conscience can't control me when I get mad.

Int.: I guess that's the real problem, isn't it, Slim? You really can't control this, even when your conscience tells you it's wrong. Seems to me that this is where you need special help.

Slim: I know it....

In this interview the goal is to stake out the problem as clearly as possible when Slim is not caught in one of his megalomaniacal episodes and to promise "lend-lease" to the superego-identified part of the ego in its struggle with the narcissitic infantile part. Obviously, there will be a need in the long-range treatment of Slim to attack many more issues than this one. Thus, the special motives and feelings into which this particular ego weakness plays and which form the central core pathology have, of course, to be dealt with. However, this narcissistic blurring of ego boundaries does stand as a formidable clinical problem on its own and there is a question as to whether entree can be gained or waited for into the deeper pathology without tackling this piece of it first. Thus, for instance, by talking with Slim about Whitey's walking habit, it was possible to explore with him the possibility that Whitey was disliked by him for still other reasons, or served as a target for other problems, and in this way Slim's pubertal, phallic competitiveness with Whitey came out. Then it was suggested to him that perhaps his dislike of Whitey's walking on his toes was based upon a fear that Whitey would leap upon him and hurt him—in this way proving he was stronger than Slim. It was interesting that this markedly paranoid boy was relieved by this "theory" which reduced his fear of Whitey. Now of course this does not cure his ego-boundary problem or his paranoia,

10

but it does aim at giving help to the uninvolved part of the ego for dealing with both if continued in balanced doses over a long enough time.

These have been some few, rough illustrations of the use of life-space interview on the level of "clinical exploitation of life events." There is no implication that a completely investigated instrument of change has been evolved or that any of the children in this setting are being treated until the correct terminal point in their therapy will have been reached. In each case, only a *piece* of the total pathology is being demonstrated as it has been contacted through the interview by picking up a life event or a series of life events packed together in a relatively short time exposure.

EMOTIONAL FIRST AID ON THE SPOT

As mentioned earlier, another major function of the life-space interview is that of simply pulling a youngster through a tight spot without any specific intention or clinical motive toward cure. Its aim is to offer to the ego hygienic protection and support which aid it in overcoming a temporary, sometimes critical, loss of function. Here, too, Redl has offered tentative categories aimed at clarifying some of the subfunctions of this style of life-space interview. Broadly, these differentiate between interviews which aid the ego in moments of (1) acute frustration, fury, guilt, or panic; (2) throw support around the ego when it is faced by sudden violent retreat from relationship; and (3) help a child steer his way safely through some complicating and confusing "social and behavioral traffic jams" and decision-making crises. For space reasons, we shall confine ourselves to samples showing two different subfunctions classifiable within these three groups. The apparent simplicity of such moments conceals their complexity and to some of our more orthodox clinical brethren may make them "undeserving" for admission to the elite status of "the interview."

INTERVIEW SUPPORT IN AN EPISODE OF PANIC

Chick, whom we have had occasion to describe a few short examples back, was watching a camp movie, "Bad Day at Black Rock," when his counselor observed him get up in a restless, agitated way and walk out of the lodge with the kind of expression that she had learned to read as "trouble." Tipped off by her I followed him out. He said nothing when I asked, "Hey, Chick, what's the trouble?" but strode purposefully along to his cabin. I jogged along by his side in as friendly and relaxed a way as I could. He got into his cabin, climbed up in a bunk, pulled up his blankets to his chin. "I ain't goin' back to that movie or the campfire later or nuthin'." "How come?" No answer. I stretched out on an empty bunk across from his, leaned back, folded my arms under my head and waited. A few minutes later, he got up just as purposefully as he had come in, pulled his blanket back, got down, strode out of the cabin. There I was again by his side. Not a word between us. He walked to the boys' "john." I waited. He came out and went back to the lodge. Instead of going in, he sat down on a bench near the door. I sat down next to him. About a minute passed. Then he said, "Some Western that is . . . no shootin' or anything!" "Oh" I said, "there'll be shootin'—wait 'till that one-armed guy catches up with the bad guy. The one that killed his buddy which is why he came to this town." "Oh," says he, "that I gotta see," and walked in. I went with him and sat by him in the movie. In a low voice I sketched out what was happening in more detail: how Spencer Tracy, the "one-armed guy," had this friend in the army who had come to this town and been killed by a gang of crooks. Some men in the town who had gone along with the killing—like a weak sheriff —had a bad conscience but were afraid to do anything about it. Now the one-armed guy was going to show them that they didn't have to be scared. He was "giving them back their guts." Then they would take care of the bad guys. Chick relaxed, exchanged comments with me, and appeared to enjoy what was happening. After a bit I "faded" away, leaving him on his own. The rest of the evening was uneventful—campfire and all.

In this encounter, Chick seems to be upset by the subtle violence of this movie as contrasted with the explicit violence of the usual Western—"ain't no shootin' or nothin'." He withdraws and finally returns after two clear-cut "regression" behaviors: climbing into bunk and urinating. In making the plot and actions *explicit* for him—like an interpretive subtitle—and throwing "proximity" protection around him, the ego is able to recontact the fear-inspiring situation and master it. This illustration would seem to be in line with Redl's category of interview helps in the management of "panic, fury, and guilt."

Is this really a "simple" situation that could have gone unhandled? Far from it! Chick, on his own, would have parlayed this momentary threat into an aggressive attack on somebody during the balance of the evening. Yet no attempt is made here to deal with any underlying causality for the ego's inability to meet this situation without fear—this is what differentiates this type of life-space interview from "clinical exploitation."

INTERVIEW SUPPORT IN MOMENTS OF "RELATIONSHIP DECAY" [13]

One of the most dangerous maneuvers of the sick ego is its tendency to draw back into the communication-bereft world of autism. While the more intactly delinquent child rarely finds this complete a retreat necessary, using mainly aggressive exploitation of the surrounding world as his major approach to all problems, there is a category of prepsychotic-like disturbances

[13] Fritz Redl, "Strategy and Techniques of the Life Space Interview," *op. cit.*

marked by explosive types of acting out intermixed with dependency and passivity, with strong superego and id forces pressing against a thin, underskilled ego, where sudden psychological retreat happens more easily than the clinician finds comfortable to behold. Such a boy was Jon, 13.

Whenever Jon became threatened by aggressive or sexual feelings regardless of whether they were set off by some action or language of other boys in the cabin or from "within" by his own feelings or fantasies, he acted like a virtual hebephrenic: cackled like a rooster, smirked, rolled his eyes, screamed wildly, attacked stronger boys recklessly, shouted obscenity. One day, after a day and a half of such behavior which was almost virtually impossible to bring under control, his whole cabin blew up at him and in their words: "We're goin' to kill the bastard!" The whole gang came in for a talk about it and in the interview room Jon continued to display the whole panorama of behavior described. Finally I asked him in a firm, decisive way: "Look, do you want to work this out or not?" He looked at me and said very calmly, "Well, Dave, you see I've been like this for three years" and then, bang! He was "off" again. Only this time he added to his previous paraphernalia of "goofiness": running out of the room, coming back, hiding under the table, getting back out again and throwing some sunflower seeds he was eating at one of the toughest kids in the cabin. Then, in response to my pressure, he would "come back again" with a few rational statements about himself and his feelings only to follow this with a fit of wildness.

After this happened about six times and it was all we could do to keep the other kids away from him, we let them go and kept him with us since it was dangerous to release him under these conditions. Dr. Phil Spielman, a visiting participating psychiatrist (on a busman's holiday from Dr. Redl's residential treatment unit at Bethesda) and known to all the boys, had been sitting in with us during the group talk and at this point said to Jon: "How come, every time you make a sensible statement about yourself, you immediately go off your rocker and act like a wild man? There is something that is bothering you but you can't come close to it without running away. Why don't you tell us what it is?" At this point I left "Phil" (as he was known to all campers) alone with Jon.

About an hour and a half later, I saw them coming down to the waterfront for a swim. Jon was literally like another person. Phil had "got to him." This particular episode, Jon had finally told Spielman, was caused by his fear of Biff, a much tougher, more primitive adolescent from a neighboring cabin who had come into Jon's cabin one day when the counselor was out for a brief while and started some rough sexual horseplay with him which involved grabbing for his genitals. Jon, quite calm now, told me later that this scared him—that he had never seen "stuff like this before." I told him I would talk to Biff and make clear that we would not tolerate anybody forcing other kids into play like that which, in my role as one of the "camp bosses," it was possible to do as far as Biff was concerned.

In this sequence of events, neither the interviewer nor I made any attempt to get at the reason as to why this upset Jon so much. This would have involved opening up on a deeper clinical level than the camp was able to engage in with Jon. The whole purpose was simply to try to get him back into communication and relationship which necessitated that he face his sexual excitement and fear that Biff had released. Also, obviously, it was important, then and there, to prove to him that we could *protect* him from Biff, which also played a decisive role in the restoration of control and the relinquishing of the bizarre borderline behavior which masked the anxiety.

In summary, these samples of "emotional first aid on the spot" type of life-space interviews are aimed at demonstrating (1) the difference between this function and "clini-cal exploitation of life events" and (2) differences between some subfunctions of the "first aid" type. It should be obvious that all the classifications of function are anything but airtight and mutually exclusive, a warning that has been stressed, right along in this discussion. For example, both Chick *and* Jon were involved in panic reactions but Jon's was of a deeper and more devastating type and threw him into a more dangerous channel of defense. The reason for subclassifying them is only to trap the different quality of challenge to the interviewer and not to imply that true compartmentalization of ego pathology and interview function really exists in a rigid sense. This same fluidity exists, as has also been stressed, between the "clinical exploitation" and "first-aid type" of interview, too, and there are many interview moments where the two major functions are converged into a single broad interview effort or alternate with each other at different time segments of the interview. This should not surprise the classicist in therapy because the same procedural fluidity exists there, too. For instance, frequently the neurotic has to be "soothed" in the very same hour as a dream is interpreted, or he has to be sympathized with or emphatically reassured of the therapist's continued affection and support even though he has death wishes toward the therapist. These are similar to the mixtures of "first aid" and "clinical exploitation" that exist on the terrain of the "life-space" approach.

Finally, it is necessary to point to a serious gap in the present discussion. Again because of space, it has not been possible to describe various critical factors that determine the ways in which the life-space interview is to be used. Issues such as *timing,* the particular *role* of the interviewer in the life of the interviewee, the *nature of the ongoing activity* within which the episode to be used for life-space interviewing may develop or even the *particular physical location* circumscribing such an event are all of vital importance. Beyond

13

offering the assurance that the relevance of all such factors is assessed in relation to each instance of use of life-space interviewing, no more can be described.

IMPLICATIONS FOR PRACTICE

What, if any, of this is translatable for general agency or outpatient clinical social work practice? The fact that life-space interviewing has been developed and tested in a relatively restricted area of institutional or quasi-institutional design and that even in such settings there is much for us to relearn and modify makes this a most speculative and tentative issue.

First, it must be clearly stated that the moment we talk about outpatient practice we should be simultaneously shifting our sites to a different type of clientele than the severely disturbed children described thus far. For them the life-space approach holds no new answers in extramural settings. There is no cheap solution for the grim lethargy of the American community in providing a tragically needed expanding front of intensive inpatient treatment designs of a variety of types for severely disturbed children and adults.

Beyond this, for appropriate practice of a clinically oriented type with properly selected clientele, one general, underlying meaning of the life-space approach would involve the development of a *tool-conscious* interest in the ongoing life experience of the client and how various segments of it may be carried into the therapeutic situation more meaningfully. We must recognize that this has been going on silently for some years in agency practice. However, since many of the life experiences of the client are made known to the worker only through the clients reporting of them, there has been reluctance to rely on these as compared to other forms of more indigenous data about the client—fantasies, fragments of emotion, attitudes toward and perceptions of the worker, behavior in the interview situation, and so on. This is a

real problem and cannot be dismissed. Still, much of what we do tactically with the client is governed by what we *believe* is achievable and reachable. If there had been no theory about the importance of dreams, no one would "dream" that such ephemeral and diffuse data could ever be recovered from the far-off corners of the psyche and converted into pragmatic materials for therapy either, and a whole magnificent skill area would not have developed. However, agency practice will, itself, have to define its adaptation of the life-space approach through appropriate experimentation and in advance of this nothing more specific should be said.

Leaving the typical agency setting and thinking of certain special, but still non-institutional designs of practice, life-space findings may hold more concrete applicatory meanings. In *detached worker* settings with the hard-to-reach and in *school social work practice,* a very clear entree for experimentation with these techniques is immediately visible. In such settings, the worker in varying ways and degrees is *already embedded in pieces of the client's life-space to begin with,* is perceived as such by the client, and has available for interview use life events in close proximity to their actual occurrence.

Finally, life-space interview findings remind us once again of the crying need for planned experimentation—and I mean in practice!—with combinations of group work and casework. What *did* happen to casework and group work as a clinical blend anyway? Fritz Redl, Gisela Konopka, and S. L. Slavson have written about it for the last twenty years, at least, in publications too numerous to mention. Yet today there is the most abject resignation in our field to the extinction of professional group work, a shaking of heads over the fact that "Group work is a dying field!" If child guidance and family casework agency practice were widened to articulate these two approaches, a badly needed gap would be filled in treatment resources for certain

14

types of problems. Although they do not require institutional therapy, clients with such problems are still not reachable without making available for treatment life experiences that can be created on the group scene and are clinically useful there as well as in the interview situation. Shall we disentomb group work?

Perhaps most fascinating—and admittedly most speculative—is one last issue: what does life-space interview suggest for a *fact and theory* base in social work? Right now our field is exhibiting a frantic lionization of the social scientist in the parlor and a frosty tolerance of the backyard romance between the kitchen maid and the local psychoanalyst on the beat. This is symptomatic of our embarrassment over having buried ourselves (and *we* did it!) too deeply in the id. There may well be an equal and opposite danger that we may, via social science, launch ourselves too swiftly into space. In either case, the client is still left in the dark where he started, poor fellow! It seems to me that life-space data suggests that in *ego processes* are wrapped up the vital connections between the person and his "inner" and "outer" worlds. The ego seems to be a continuum with one end buried (but alive and "kicking"!) in the slumbering roots of the person and the other proliferated into a sensitive network involved in sleepless radarlike contact with the world around it. The resultant picture is that of an enormous, multifunctional plasticity about which we still know pitifully little. This is where we have found—in the "life-space circuit"—our most fascinating clinical challenge. Obviously, we have had to become involved most elaborately with special features—social and nonsocial—of the environmental terrain. However, *the ego is not its environment,* not even that part that becomes specialized for the task of dealing with it. It is always "attached" to the person who "carries" it—even when its "radar" is madly clicking in space with varying, and variable, influences from without.

In our "knowledge rush" toward social science, are we remembering that ego function is a *personal* function? The gap between the data of social science and individual psychology is by no means closed and it is treacherously possible to intermingle carelessly perceptions arising from these two discrete modes of observation and description. The view, for example, that the proper goal of social work is the "enhancement of social functioning" already seems to carry an imagery leaning toward peace with the offerings (and critiques of social work!) of social science. The auxiliary concepts that are lined up with this goal-concept: *role, interaction, environment,* also speak out for this orientation. What is the view of the person that is coming out of this? It is a view of man as *social-man* as opposed to *id-man.* Ego psychology will not, in a manner of speaking, "have" this. The ego—as a function of mind—is no more "loyal" to social-man than it is to id-man. In short, the type of involvement that social work is developing with social science may leave us—as did our handling of psychoanalysis—with a *half-man.* It portends a violation of the concept of the *total person.* If, as seems to be the case, a smooth conceptual model for the determinants of the total person are not yet deducible from social science and individual psychology, this is our proper cross to bear and, operationally speaking, our practical functioning in relation to the client world must reflect, clumsy though it may seem, a tortuous fidelity to two oracles instead of one.

15

BY ROBERT SUNLEY

New Dimensions in Reaching-out Casework

■ *How can casework expand its framework and develop methods of helping the many people, especially among the poor, who do not voluntarily come to social agencies for help and who do not respond to conventional approaches? The author discusses new ways of reaching out to such people, as experimented with by the Family Service Association of Nassau County, Mineola, New York, which include the nonproblem approach, "situational" casework, and "cognitive" casework.* ■

IN THE PAST fifteen years, agencies and caseworkers have experimented with a variety of methods to help those who seldom appear voluntarily within agency premises. It has been recognized that many people in need of some kind of service do not come forward with formulated problems to obtain help. The efforts to reach people and establish treatment relationships with them have become known as "reaching-out" or aggressive casework.

Certain subgroups of those who need help, it is true, have received considerable attention: the multiproblem family, the hard to reach, and the school dropout, for example. The number of programs for such groups has run into the many hundreds, at least, involving many individual casework programs as well as broad-scale efforts aimed at whole sections of a city.[1]

Yet most within this large population have remained unserved or underserved. Professional casework agencies, and especially family agencies, have been aware of this lack but have not been able to com-

mand the financial resources and trained staff to expand their efforts significantly. With the advent of broad community development programs in large cities, and even more so with the initiation of poverty programs throughout the country, casework was regarded as having failed the poor and deprived. From the federal down to the local level, opinions have been expressed to the effect that casework reaches too few poor people, is too time consuming, too expensive, and—most serious of all—largely ineffectual.[2]

From quite a new quarter has come another challenge. The poor are culturally deprived or, more accurately, cognitively deprived, according to many recent studies. Is this a field only for the educators and social psychologists, or do caseworkers have a part to play in it? Are there ways in which

ROBERT SUNLEY, MSW, *is Assistant Director, Family Service Association of Nassau County, Mineola, New York.*

[1] Joseph C. Lagey and Beverly Ayres, "Community Treatment Programs for Multi-Problem Families" (Vancouver, B.C.: Research Department, Community Chest and Councils of the Greater Vancouver Area, 1962). (Mimeographed.)

[2] *See,* for example, Richard A. Cloward, "Social Class and Private Social Agencies," *Proceedings,* Eleventh Annual Program Meeting, Boston, Massachusetts (New York: Council on Social Work Education, 1963), pp. 123–137.

Reprinted from SOCIAL WORK, 13 (April 1968), pp. 64–74. Copyright © by the National Association of Social Workers, Inc., 1968.

CAO–006–C

casework can incorporate help for cognitive deprivation without abandoning the principles of casework?

These challenges lead caseworkers to look more deeply into casework itself, to find fresh approaches or new dimensions that can bridge the gap between the known needs and the sources of help. To do this, they need to suspend conventional notions of motivation, problems, and treatment. As William H. Key put it: "We turned the usual clinical situation upside down." [3]

By conceptualizing, developing, and planfully using new outlooks or dimensions in casework, further diagnostic and treatment methods for individuals and groups may be discovered, agency programs can be better formulated and carried out, and social work as a profession can move away from the tendency—not unique to social work—to cast blame on the clientele as "unmotivated" or "resistant." These attitudes would be true enough if measured by the bureaucratic demands that clients appear at centrally located offices at specified intervals and behave in certain ways in an interview. But if we as social workers take a broader view and ask: "How can we extend help to such people?" we must reconstruct our own approaches through studying our failures and omissions. *We* can do it; the potential client cannot or does not.

The three dimensions described here— the nonproblem approach, situational casework, and cognitive casework—are not the only ones being experimented with at present. A new dimension in personnel, for example, is represented by the use of indigenous aides in work with the poor; it has been developed in Mobilization For Youth and other pilot programs, used widely in Community Action Programs (CAP's) sponsored by the Office of Economic Opportunity, and adapted further

in Project ENABLE. Yet another dimension might be a secondary therapeutic use of primarily nontherapeutic groups (such as community action groups), under the leadership or co-leadership of a caseworker, in which the now random beneficial effects on individual personality could be used purposively by the caseworker, perhaps as one component of an over-all treatment plan. [4]

TRADITIONAL REACHING OUT

In the traditional aggressive or reaching-out casework, the caseworker knocks on the family's door, brought there by a problem that has been perceived by a community agency or professional. [5] His entrée *is* the problem, however politely couched or disguised. The family, in turn, perceives that he has come because of a problem, which they must acknowledge or deny. The stage for casework is set in this problem orientation. While some unquestioned successes have resulted, most professionals realize that the problem-oriented method has considerable limitations. For example, in families approached for treatment through aggressive casework, one finding was the following:

In the first place, it was frequently difficult to make even initial contact with referred cases, a considerable proportion of whom never were seen or were seen only once or twice. Second, achieving involvement in casework was difficult or impossible, even when contact was made. The customary approaches to establishing relationships through regular casework interviews did not seem effective. [6]

[3] William H. Key, "Controlled Intervention— The Helping Professions and Directed Social Change," *American Journal of Orthopsychiatry,* Vol. 36, No. 3 (April 1966), p. 406.

[4] Rudolph M. Wittenberg, "Personality Adjustment Through Social Action," *American Journal of Orthopsychiatry,* Vol. 18, No. 2 (March 1958), pp. 207–221.

[5] Alice Overton, "Serving Families Who 'Don't Want Help,'" *Social Casework,* Vol. 34, No. 7 (July 1953), pp. 304–309.

[6] Henry J. Meyer, Edgar F. Borgatta, and Wyatt C. Jones, *Girls at Vocational High* (New York: Russell Sage Foundation, 1965), p. 17.

2

Another effort, conducted by a family agency in a large city, reported:

> . . . we seemed to be unable to reach these families through either the giving of money or the usual casework interviews. Our early efforts were directed toward helping the client focus his problems. These efforts largely failed. Either the client could not articulate his problems at all or he could not do so at the level expected of him. . . . Neither was ordinary empathy with the family productive.[7]

In brief, many families fail to respond to such an approach, many superficially comply but fail to show any change, and many are not approached because no one has officially complained about them. Problem-oriented reaching-out casework, then, offers one method but is not a comprehensive one for all families. How then to reach the many others?

Moving beyond the problem-oriented approach, one may think next of reaching clients through allied services: camps, day care, homemaker services, legal advisory services, consumer credit services, and the like. While these are unquestionably important in themselves, for the caseworker they are peripheral to the central problems of family relationships and conflicts. It would appear that such approaches, whether initiated by the client or. agency, should lead into the heart of family problems, so that the relationship thus established can be used as the basis for moving in on family problems. Sometimes this does occur but workers have had many frustrating experiences in trying to involve such clients in casework. Too often the potential client slips away, apparently unmotivated for further help; others are seen

occasionally as a need arises, only to break the peripherally established contact again.

NONPROBLEM APPROACH

The idea of a nonproblem approach is implicit in the very formulation of a problem-oriented approach. What would it consist of and has it been tried?

Obviously, the client and worker must meet on neutral ground, so to speak. The basis of their contacts initially must not focus on the client's problems, nor even threaten to do so. Potential continuity of contact, flexibility, and availability of the worker are also called for. The agency philosophy and structure must permit time to be spent that cannot be categorized formally and statistically as interviews. Families must be regarded not as cases that are opened and closed but as *people* remaining in some kind of contact with workers and agency. The agency must build a permissive setting in which the client may at some point talk about personal problems but is not required to. The client then talks when motivated; it is not the *agency's* motivation that produces the significant encounter between client and worker. It is this very lack of motivation of the client that has been a major obstacle in rendering help to the disadvantaged. The client, in the problem-oriented approach, does not select the difficulty for which help is wanted or the grounds and terms on which it is given. A nonproblem approach reverses this situation. It avoids resorting to more aggression in pursuing families who appear unmotivated.

The nonproblem approach, then, usually would require a local or neighborhood base, in which client and worker meet each other in a variety of ways. The agency would be there for reasons beyond (but including) help for family problems, and the worker would become a perceptible part of the daily lives of the local people. More and more people would be reached in some way. Community centers, settlement houses,

---

[7] Kenneth Dick and Lydia J. Strnad, "The Multi-Problem Family and Problems of Service," *Social Casework*, Vol. 39, No. 6 (June 1958), p. 354. *See also, Working With the Poor*, Report of a Three-Year Consultation Service—Public Housing (Syracuse, N.Y.: Syracuse University, Youth Development Center, 1965), p. 35.

and multiservice centers under CAP's all potentially provide such a setting. Few, however, are set up as integrated services, in which casework is not a separate "department" to which people are referred in the usual manner. Such settings can, with the concept of the nonproblem approach, be adapted to take advantage of this additional method of reaching out.

To illustrate the nonproblem approach, the following example is taken from the Family Community Center of the Youth Service Project, a setting reconceptualized to approximate more closely the nonproblem approach.[8]

Mrs. C, 34, and her husband, 36, had resisted all efforts at help by welfare, probation, public health, public school, and other agencies, although always polite and agreeable when contacted. The center caseworkers and group workers had "peripheral" contacts around summer day camp, registration for group work, and the like for the children, ages 5, 7, 11, and 14. Pooling of information indicated serious family problems: Mr. C was an alcoholic, their teen-ager an unapprehended delinquent, the next two children evidenced behavior and learning problems. The family was little known in the community, being rather seclusive. Eventually a contact with Mrs. C was made through the one neighbor she talked with who brought her to a meeting of the Auxiliary, a group of mothers who met at the center to provide refreshments, party decorations, and so forth for children's groups. Mrs. C attended several meetings at which the caseworker was present, and one time expressed interest in obtaining a recipe mentioned by her. The next day the caseworker dropped by to give it to her. After two more such visits, the caseworker was detained by Mrs. C, who introduced the subject of her husband's abusiveness

toward her and whether she should continue to tolerate it.

While such an approach seems simple, in practice it develops out of the concept of the nonproblem approach. The essential element is the existence of a setting within which the client can finally apply for help out of his own motivation, when he is ready, and for a problem concerning him, not the community. While caseworkers have in the past certainly shown great ingenuity in overcoming resistance and suspiciousness in somewhat similar ways, the problem-oriented approach necessarily leaves the client still unmotivated; resistance and fear may be lulled so that the client will acknowledge problems but yet not really ask for help.

A second example illustrates how an unsuccessful problem-oriented approach was reformulated with the nonproblem orientation.[9]

The problem of young unwed mothers came daily to the attention of the family caseworkers. It was decided to form a group of such girls, all on welfare. Despite strenuous efforts, the caseworker could not get more than one or two girls to come to a meeting. The local neighborhood aides suggested the girls might resent being categorized in this way, and might not see illegitimacy as a problem per se.

By applying the nonproblem approach, the staff then developed a plan to hold meetings in one of two apartment buildings in which many of the residents were unwed mothers. Films, discussions, and refreshments would be offered, with efforts made to involve all residents in eventually talking about their everyday difficulties.

Within a nonproblem setting both the problem and peripheral approaches can

[8] The Youth Service Project in Freeport, New York, is conducted by Family Service Association of Nassau County and is co-sponsored by the Nassau County Youth Board and the New York State Division for Youth.

[9] The example is drawn from the Multi-Service Center in Glen Cove, New York, which was operated in 1965–66 by Family Service Association of Nassau County under contract with the Glen Cove Economic Opportunity Council.

4

and may have to be used at times, especially in certain emergencies, but probably more effectively together than in isolation. The client seems to experience the agency and worker as less of a threat or an alien intrusion into the community and family.

Another technique in the nonproblem approach is *reporting*. The caseworker visits parents at intervals to report how their children are doing in a center activity or to advise them of other planned activities. Again, the nonthreatening approach permits contacts to develop slowly into a beginning relationship. These and similar meetings (such as park bench conversations) are recorded statistically as *significant contacts* in the Youth Service Project as a way of formally according importance to this aspect of the caseworker's activity.

The nonproblem approach may blur the sharp distinctions between types of social workers. All may share to some extent in the generalized role of community worker but retain their specialized areas as well. The caseworker finds himself at times in ambiguous roles, not quite a caseworker, group worker, or community organizer. He may lead a group that is not quite group therapy, yet not a group work group, a recreational group, or a community action group. The nature of the group evolves out of the immediate needs of certain people, perceived and developed by the caseworker.

> The caseworker, with his office near the door of the center, found himself about to behave as a policeman by chasing away a group of about eight boys, ages 7 to 10, who threw bottles and created other annoyances on evenings when teenage groups were meeting in the center. True, they were all eligible to join in their own age group activities in the afternoon, when such children are supposed to be engaged in groups—but not at 9:00 P.M.! Turning the situation around, the caseworker asked himself: "What do they want?" and shortly found himself conducting an early evening group of children who had no other place

to go and who could begin to make their real needs known once their outcry had been acknowledged.

The nonproblem dimension has emerged from the multiservice neighborhood setting. Does it have applicability for the family agency or other problem-oriented casework agency? Could unreached members of the middle-class and blue collar groups be reached in this way? In order to implement these ideas the agency must first develop a strong commitment to devote part of its resources to reaching the unreached of a socioeconomic group. Second, the caseworker must help translate this philosophy into imaginative efforts that will, in effect, open up the four walls of the office into the community. Where and how can the agency and caseworker position themselves differently to be available when the unreached clientele become motivated?

SITUATIONAL CASEWORK

Another new dimension in reaching-out casework relates to the role of the caseworker and client in the client's actual life situations.[10] Usually, casework is reportive and vicarious; the caseworker hears about what has happened or is going to happen. He understands empathically and helps the client to express feelings and thoughts before and after an event. The following two case studies illustrate how the same event can be handled in two ways, first in the vicarious manner, then in the situational manner.

> On Monday in the office Mrs. A tells the caseworker she is going to visit her adolescent son, George, who was com-

---

[10] The initial formulation of this concept was made by Mrs. Mildred Reed of the Nassau County Department of Public Welfare, when a graduate student at the agency. An exact adjective to describe this type of casework was difficult to find; such terms as "participant" or "experiential" have misleading connotations. "Situational" was chosen to indicate that the client and worker are *in the situation*, not jointly talking about it.

mitted two months before to a mental hospital. She visited him several times but now has an appointment with the hospital social worker to "give a history." Her caseworker tries to elicit what she thinks will happen, but Mrs. A, although obviously nervous, cannot verbalize any specific concerns. She agrees to return the next week to talk about her visit. In the next interview, she relates that the social worker at the hospital asked a lot of questions, mostly about the family members' age, residence, education, and the like. She also waited to talk with the doctor, hoping to be told the results of some tests. Neither doctor nor social worker apparently gave her any information. Mrs. A rather confusedly expressed anger, which the caseworker thought to be of a slightly paranoid flavor. Because of Mrs. A's touchiness, he could not question her in sufficient detail to determine what had actually happened. She, on the other hand, left with a comment that the caseworker probably correctly interpreted as meaning he did not understand her very well.

. . . . .

Mrs. A telephoned (an unusual occurrence) to ask the caseworker to accompany her to the hospital. She explained that she needed transportation by car, and the caseworker agreed. When he called for her she showed him her appointment slip to see the hospital social worker. "Did she want him to be present?" "Yes, she would feel better." She also explained that she wanted to try once more to see the doctor and they discussed her prior efforts to do so. At the hospital, after some waiting, the two were shown into the social worker's office. Routinely he rattled off questions, not pausing to notice Mrs. A's reactions or to pursue certain implications in her statements. He waved aside her request for information on tests given her son; only the doctor could say anything. "Could she see the doctor?" "Maybe."

Two hours later, Mrs. A and the caseworker located the doctor, who was understandably busy (although Mrs. A noticed and commented on various per-

sonnel who spent much of that time drinking coffee and chatting). The doctor, although not unfriendly, could tell her nothing; he politely suggested it was too soon to reach any conclusions. (Only two weeks later George was suddenly released from the hospital.) On the way home, the caseworker had no difficulty in getting Mrs. A to express feelings about how she had been treated. Having seen how she was treated, he did not suspect any paranoid leanings but instead learned that she tended to blame herself and excuse others, minimizing what had actually happened. Probably Mrs. A had needed the caseworker's presence, not to intervene for her (which he did not do), but instead to be a witness who could confirm what she suspected but was too uncertain to verbalize.

This second type of casework is thus one in which the caseworker is present during a client's actual life experience. He is not a real participant in the experience as a member of the family would be; it is a professional experience for him. But the client experiences him much differently than in the office setting—they both have a common reality to refer to, with all the richness of detail and subtleties mutually experienced or perceived. The client can test his perception against the caseworker's, gaining assurance that he is not "crazy," mistaken, or inferior.

The previous example illustrates one kind of situational casework in which the worker's role is primarily focused on therapeutic concerns. Another broad category, already used to some extent in casework, is the *problem-solving* role. The caseworker intervenes actively in the situation, mainly as a supplementary "ego" to enable the client to solve the immediate problem. Often the worker becomes the client's advocate, with the possible danger of taking over from the client. The problem-solving role is obviously indicated in certain critical situations when the welfare of the client and his family is actually at stake. At other times, however, the therapeutic focus clearly

6

is preferable in that it helps the client move toward independence.

The appropriateness of situational casework for reaching out to the broad group of clientele already described is obvious. For clients who are guarded or suspicious, who have difficulty in verbalizing and conceptualizing in vicarious casework, who are uncertain of their own perceptions, who fear to appear critical or ungrateful, situational casework seems indicated as one method to be used. It is questionable whether it would ever be an exclusive tool in treatment, but it can be a valuable means of intervention at selected points of treatment. It may also provide an opening from which to begin vicarious casework, either initially or after a period of unsuccessful vicarious casework.[11]

Home visits might seem to be examples of situational casework—have caseworkers not always done that? Although some home visits might turn out to be situational, routine home visits are usually vicarious in that the client is reporting events. But if the alcoholic husband returns home during the visit and a fight ensues, the caseworker is unquestionably in a situation! What makes it situational casework, however, is not merely the physical presence of the caseworker, but the conscious and planned use of the joint situational experience as a way to reach and involve the client.

Situational casework need not be solely and fortuitously initiated by the client, of course. The caseworker may work toward a joint development of a situational experience, responding to the client's need. For example, a youth expressing the wish to get a job was accompanied to the employment center and to the place of employment, with the specific suggestion of going there having originated with the caseworker. Other examples of situational casework would include the worker accompanying the client to a department store when an important purchase is to be made or to the library to introduce it to the client and her child.

Two questions arise: "Have caseworkers not always done such things?" "Will the client not be infantilized?" Caseworkers, it is true, have acted similarly, although perhaps they have not often deliberately done what is here defined as situational casework. Often they have done things for clients, have prepared them to do things, and have interceded with agencies on their behalf.

Some caseworkers accompany clients to key interviews, but usually as their allies, not to view the situation as the equivalent of a casework interview. The conceptualization of situational casework may help to sanction the caseworker's activity because his participation in such situations has often been frowned on in the past, considered menial and to be relegated to case aides or volunteers, if possible, or at best considered a necessary evil that interferes with vicarious casework.

In practice, situational casework may be considered to encompass a broader range of activities than a strict definition might indicate. The concept itself is suggestive of different approaches with people. Even within the agency premises, situational casework (more broadly conceived) could take place. As a hypothetical example, a group of mothers and their preschool children come into a large playroom to test out new play materials, with the caseworker not only observing but taking part in activities between mother and child, child and child, and mother and mother. While such a situation may be artificially initiated, a transition occurs in which it seems to become a real life experience for the clients.

Is the client being infantilized? Is dependency being encouraged? The caseworker partly determines this through his handling of himself. Much verbal intervention by the caseworker into a situation would tend to rob the client of the strength-

11 Ethel J. Panter, "Ego-building Procedures that Foster Social Functioning," *Social Casework,* Vol. 47, No. 3 (March 1966), pp. 139–145.

7

ening aspects of the experience, just as taking only the problem-solving role would do. But situational casework is not intervention in this sense. An analogy could be made to a conventional casework interview in which a client "borrows ego" from the worker and goes away to use it in real life. In situational casework, the worker supplies a comparable support for a client who does not hold onto such help easily away from the worker's presence.

And, partly, the question itself reflects the "crutch" philosophy—the fear of making people dependent on caseworkers. Yet for the culturally deprived client who is able to see vicarious casework as no more than a vehicle for direct advice, as intercession with authorities, as concrete aid of various kinds, situational casework may provide a breakthrough for caseworker and client. An experience with it might, for example, be followed up the next time by role-playing a forthcoming experience in the office or home setting—a once-removed type of situational casework. As has been pointed out, role-playing with such clientele is often highly effective.[12]

COGNITIVE CASEWORK

Cognitive deficiency, a term little known in casework, broadly refers to the lacks many people suffer in the normal development of their thinking processes. For the most part, although not exclusively, such deficits occur among the poor regardless of nationality or race. Perhaps of most significance for caseworkers, the results of cognitive deficits (or cultural deprivation) are rather constant despite the individual's emotional condition. Help with emotional problems, then, whether the client is 4 or 40, does not appear sufficient to overcome such handicaps. It has been pointed out that such

deficits seriously impair the young child's development of rational thought and self-control.

A wide range of difficulties result from cognitive deficits that are obviously enmeshed with concurrent and/or resulting emotional problems as well. Many of the characteristics ascribed to the poor, such as apathy, hopelessness, indifference; inability to plan, to generalize from experience, to master academic or abstract subjects, and the like are at least partly related to cognitive deficits.[13] Recent research has pinpointed certain areas of deficiency fairly well, such as auditory and visual discrimination, memory, language use, classification, and symbolic thinking. Massive preventive and remedial intervention is needed and is partially under way now in this country, as demonstrated by the Head Start programs.

Does casework have any part to play in this vast area of human development and growth? It would be easy to answer: "No, let casework stick to its own field." Unfortunately, no one problem area is neatly isolated from all others. Those who do casework with the disadvantaged cannot stay away from the causes and consequences of cognitive deficits, which seem to be part and parcel of the vast complex of causes and results culminating in the far-spreading disturbances of many families that have been handed down from one generation to the next. Nor does it seem reasonable for the caseworker to help a family with one problem area while ignoring another one equally vital to over-all family and individual development. Education in the

12 Frank Riessman and Jean Goldfarb, "Role Playing and the Poor," in Frank Riessman, Jerome Cohen, and Arthur Pearl, eds., *Mental Health of the Poor* (New York: Free Press of Glencoe, 1964), pp. 336–347.

13 Compare Vera John, "The Intellectual Development of Slum Children: Some Preliminary Findings," *American Journal of Orthopsychiatry*, Vol. 33, No. 5 (October 1963), pp. 813–822; Jerome Siller, "Socio-economic Status and Conceptual Thinking," *Journal of Abnormal and Social Psychology*, Vol. 55 (1957), pp. 365–371; and Martin Deutsch, "The Disadvantaged Child and the Learning Process," in A. Harry Passow, ed., *Education in Depressed Areas* (New York: Teachers Press, Teachers College, Columbia University, 1963), pp. 163–179.

8

usual sense is not enough, for it can hardly reach those who feel hopeless; are unmotivated, easily frustrated or defeated, depressed, and unable to make such a large and risky investment in the future. Nor does education, at least as now conducted, touch on the early-level deficits, which are the basic tools or skills necessary for thinking, academic learning, and everyday living. Nor can educational methods help eliminate the emotional problems also standing in the way.

Approaching the problem from another angle, casework is concerned with the broad area of ego psychology. Helping a person with cognitive deficits would then fall well within the area of ego support and ego strengthening. In fact, a good part of casework is concerned with this area of personality. For example, helping a client to see alternative solutions, to formulate a problem so it can be discussed, and to observe more closely what happens at home are part of the casework method. This level of casework is usually too abstract and complex for the client who suffers from the basic cognitive deficits common among the poor. But is there not good reason for caseworkers to gear their approaches to helping people at their appropriate level?

If the validity of casework concerning itself with cognitive deficits in some way is accepted, the next question is, "How?" The worker cannot guide an adult client through steps in visual and auditory discrimination on the most elementary level. Clients would probably feel insulted, unable to comprehend what value they would receive, or lack the motivation to embark on such a program. In short, adults cannot be asked to prepare themselves to enter nursery school. Nor would it be correct to view them as children; they are adults with certain disabilities.

Casework has some marked advantages in working with the culturally deprived. One is the establishment of the one-to-one relationship on which further efforts can be built. Another asset is the working

knowledge of people's feelings and underlying attitudes, their defensive systems, and their symptomatology. The caseworker can proceed from a diagnostic assessment geared to the individual, not to a class as in education.

Taking the above assets and drawbacks into account, the preliminary thinking of the Youth Service Project staff became directed toward a group that seemed likely to respond to some type of cognitive casework—the mothers of young children. Using the concept that the helper is often aided as much as the target for help, it was decided to enlist the mothers of 2-year-olds to help their children, but with the ultimate aim of helping *both* cognitively.[14]

Studies have shown, for example, that the lower-class Negro infant seems to develop normally, in terms of cognition and motor capacity, until he is 2 years old.[15] Between then and the time he enters school, the young child falls seriously behind the middle-class child. The cognitive deficits occur during this brief but critical formative period.

Also, "cultural deprivation," the term in current usage (in place of "cognitive deficits") has led to misunderstandings of the meaning of "cultural" and to remedial efforts that were designed to provide more and varied experiences or to enrichment programs for disadvantaged children. But as has been pointed out by Hess and Shipman:

. . . enrichment for the sake of enrichment may miss the point—that it is not additional or even more varied stimula-

14 Frank Riessman, "The 'Helper' Therapy Principle" (New York: Mobilization For Youth, 1963). (Mimeographed.)

15 Hilda Knoblock and Benjamin Pasamanick, "Further Observations on the Behavioral Development of Negro Children," *Journal of Genetic Psychology*, Vol. 83 (1953), pp. 137–157; Nancy Bayley, "Comparisons of Mental and Motor Test Scores for Ages One to Fifteen Months by Sex, Birth Order, Race, Geographic Location, and Education of Parents," *Child Development*, Vol. 36, No. 2 (June 1965), pp. 379–411.

9

tion that is needed, but experiences which give stimuli a pattern of sequential meaning.[16]

An experimental program was developed from this thinking and was then worked out by a consulting psychologist, to be carried out by caseworkers with a experimental and control group subjected to pre- and posttesting.

Each caseworker was assigned three mothers and their respective 2-year-olds, selected at random from the total group; all were of low socioeconomic status; all had indicated interest. On the first of two weekly visits, the caseworker brought a toy or similar Verbal Interaction Stimulus Material (VISM) to the home and spent time with the child and mother in using it, emphasizing the verbalization that can take place between them around the child's use of the object. (The VISM's are selected to focus on elementary cognitive steps, such as naming and simple classifying, coupled with motor activity.) The worker also brought a simple book, which she demonstrated. Both objects were left with the family permanently. On the second visit that week, the caseworker brought another toy but not a book. (All VISM's are selected and scaled both for increasing complexity and for lending themselves to and encouraging language use.) During the discussion, the worker encouraged the mother and child to bring out and review prior VISM's and inquired about their usage. By focusing positive verbal attention on cognitive aspects of the child's play and verbalization, she also used a reinforcement technique of operant conditioning, i.e., reward by attention.

Without going into further details of this project, which showed statistically significant results, it can be noted that the caseworker intervened not only in the area of cognitive deficits but also in that of the

---

[16] Robert D. Hess and Virginia Shipman, "Early Blocks to Children's Learning," *Children,* Vol. 12, No. 5 (September–October 1965), p. 194.

mother's self-image. The responsiveness, flexibility, and relatedness required of the caseworkers point also to the validity of their performing such activities. They must assess each mother's degree of emotional disturbance (one or two in the project could have been diagnosed as psychotic) and determine how to handle manifestations of the disturbance.

Thus far, the focus has been primarily on the children's cognitive deficits and the possible methods to offset them. What of the adults, the parents? As yet, no specific casework programs seem to have been attempted. An intra-agency memorandum of the Family Service Association of Nassau County was addressed to a program of cognitive casework with adults, pointing out some key concepts and suggesting possible casework programs.

1. Culturally deprived adults seem to be impaired in concepts of causality and time. They have much difficulty in transferring and developing what they have learned in one situation to another somewhat similar one. At the same time, the immediate environment does not require, nor even stimulate, the constant use and further development of conceptual powers.

2. Two critical areas of cognitive deficit—time and causality—may be related to two major areas of emotional problems —depression and impulsiveness or acting out. While the cognitive deficits would presumably remain if a depression were lifted, is it possible that lessening the cognitive deficits could lead to a lessening of depression and/or impulsiveness?

3. The life situations with which the caseworker tries to help are highly complex (from a conceptual point of view) and emotionally charged. It does not seem likely that any method can be introduced *within* the casework interview that would operate at a beginning level conceptually but at the same time meet the needs and demands of life situations. This suggests the need for separate, concurrent types of interviews or sessions.

4. Methods of approach might include

individual casework sessions concurrent with sessions focused on cognitive deficits; family sessions, perhaps similarly structured; and group meetings of parents or of people assembled for projects or tasks, in which focus on the thinking processes was emphasized.

5. An initial evaluation through testing would have to be made of each individual, to determine areas of cognitive deficit.

6. Several critical questions must then be thought out: How do we present such a program to a client? Does the same caseworker conduct both types of sessions? What would be the content of the cognitive sessions?

The last question is obviously the most difficult and important. In the last few years research in the field of cognitive development has produced some knowledge that may serve as guidelines, but there is no definitive body of accepted knowledge that can be adapted to casework. Yet caseworkers need not wait for the final refinements in this field (as they cannot in other areas as well). Certainly, one avenue of approach would be to use materials and experiences from the client's familiar environment as the basic ingredients of a cognitive session. Other more suitable approaches could undoubtedly be devised, but it would seem important to make a start and to evaluate what is done with sufficient precision so that some positive or negative knowledge emerges.

SUMMARY

Under the pressure of new programs and knowledge, caseworkers are challenged to examine more radically ways and methods of serving a large portion of the population previously characterized as unmotivated, untreatable, or unreachable. Three new dimensions or ways of reaching out are described:

1. The nonproblem approach, in which the worker-client relationship is first developed on a basis unrelated to family problems, thus giving the client freedom to determine which of his problems he will discuss and when.

2. Situational casework, in which the worker is present in certain life situations of the client, assuming an ego-supportive role with either a therapeutic or problem-solving focus.

3. Cognitive casework, as a new facet in the ego-strengthening function of casework, directed toward lessening the cognitive deficiencies of the socially disadvantaged population.

These and other new approaches briefly mentioned provide new programs and therapeutic approaches for planful use by agencies and practitioners. Adaptation by family agencies represents a further challenge and difficulty, in order to utilize the centralized casework office setups common to most family agencies.

CAO–006–C

BY GERALD M. SHATTUCK AND JOHN M. MARTIN

New Professional Work Roles and Their Integration into a Social Agency Structure

■ *The experience of a demonstration program designed to prevent pupils from dropping out of school points to the complex roles social workers must assume to deal with the social structure and institutions. The paper is divided into three parts: (1) a description of the new work roles that emerged from the program, (2) a discussion of the relationship between these new roles and agency structure, and (3) four conclusions that relate to future program planning in social welfare.* ■

THIS PAPER TAKES as its point of departure the evolution of a demonstration program designed to prevent pupils from dropping out of school in New York City. The demonstration program provided the empirical experience from which several more general social work policy issues arose. Emphasis is placed on the emergence of new professional work roles that were found necessary to meet the school dropout problem and the mediating role of welfare in dealing with the undereducation of the disadvantaged in public schools. The analysis is divided into three parts: (1) a description of the emergence of new work roles in the program, (2) a discussion of the relationship between new work roles and agency structure, and (3) four conclusions that seem relevant to more general program planning in social welfare in the future.

CASE IN POINT

A clear example of the complexities of the school dropout problem is found in the experiences of a six-year (1965–71) demonstration project being conducted by the Educational Alliance on the Lower East Side of New York City, in co-operation with the New York City Board of Education.[1] The program involves the efforts of a team of four social workers to help 120 adolescent enrollees deal more effectively with their school-related problems. Its aim is to prevent the participants from leaving school prematurely and in that way provide them with more adequate education and the capacity for better future employment. The staff is supported by part-time graduate students in social work and by consultants from the fields of sociology, psychology, and social work.

The program was initially structured around group counseling, regular meetings with enrollees' parents, academic remediation, and guided work experience.[2] School

GERALD M. SHATTUCK, Ph.D., *is Assistant Professor of Sociology, and* JOHN M. MARTIN, Ed.D., *is Professor of Sociology, Department of Sociology and Anthropology, Fordham University, Bronx, New York.*

[1] The Educational Alliance is a nonprofit community agency with a long history of social action work in New York City. The present project is funded by the Social and Rehabilitation Service, U.S. Department of Health, Education, and Welfare project titled "An After School Work and Counseling Program for Potential Dropouts in a Low Income Neighborhood."

[2] For a more detailed outline of the program's structure *see* Dan Rubenstein, Sol Sobsey, and Gerald M. Shattuck, "Preventing High School Dropouts," *Rehabilitation Record*, Vol. 7, No. 4 (July–August 1966), pp. 22–24.

Reprinted from SOCIAL WORK, 14 (July 1969), pp. 13–20. Copyright © by the National Association of Social Workers, Inc., 1969.

CAO–007–C

authorities provided the pool of cases from which program participants were selected. This pool was composed of youths who were suffering from one or more problems related to school performance, such as low school grades, truancy, poor reading and mathematics scores, and inappropriate behavior patterns. These problems were held to represent a syndrome of deviant behavior in most cases.

The children, mainly Puerto Rican and Negro, reside in a low-income neighborhood and the majority live in public housing projects. When selected in 1965, they were attending a local junior high school. Sixty were selected from the seventh grade and sixty from the ninth grade. The grade split was arranged so that a variable response to the program by age and grade could be observed. Ten groups of students were formed, which were segregated by sex. (Each group was composed of twelve students.) Membership in the program was, of course, voluntary, and parents were consulted regarding their children's participation.

A weekly stipend was paid to the enrollees to provide them with pocket money as well as to motivate them to persist in what, for many, was presumed to be a difficult and trying school experience. The program has been operating for over four years and so far one child who had originally enrolled while in the seventh grade and twelve who had enrolled while in the ninth grade are known to have been discharged from school.

NEW PROFESSIONAL WORK ROLES

In addition to demonstrating a capacity for keeping likely dropouts in school, the program has succeeded in uncovering a number of problems associated with early school-leaving. These problems point up the complex roles that project staff must play in dealing with the children, parents, and school personnel in the project. The following are several significant examples of the types of new roles that were assumed:

Conveners, mediators, and interpreters. During discussion meetings early in the program, several parents expressed fear, distrust, and frustration that resulted from their dealings with school authorities. One parent suggested that a meeting be arranged between parents and the school staff on neutral ground (at a local neighborhood center) and that the project's staff be present. During the meeting, parents raised a variety of questions, including the availability of career guidance counselors, the meaning of school grades, and the nature of basic school policies regarding the treatment of their children. The staff members found themselves involved in three work roles that were new in terms of the project's initial orientation: (1) They were acting as conveners, i.e., they were, by calling together two parties to a community problem (the parents and school staff), providing a new framework for the resolution of an old problem. (2) While in this role, the staff members found that they were relatively neutral to the problem and thus were able to mediate between the two parties. (Furthermore, both parties trusted the staff implicitly, which was shown by the fact that they consented to come to the meeting.) (3) To the extent that subcultural and other differences existed between the two parties, staff workers became aware of their role as interpreters. Thus, they were able to explain to each party something of the other's frame of reference so that a fuller understanding of apparently conflicting viewpoints was achieved. In playing these roles, the staff members were able to help parents relate more effectively to their children's school.

Advocates. In some cases, project youths had trouble with the police and courts or were on the verge of suspension from school. In these situations, the staff members found themselves in the role of advocate. Thus, they have represented the children when no other adequate defense was forthcoming.

Both Grosser and Cloward and Piven indicate the need for advocacy on behalf

2

of otherwise defenseless clients.[3] Taking the same tack, Briar warns social workers against defining the caseworker as simply a therapist; he should, for example, be just as much a social reformer, depending on the client's needs.[4] More specifically, Constance Baker Motley, a federal district court judge in New York City, decided in 1967 that children have the right to an attorney at school suspension hearings.[5] The results of a survey of project staff indicate their agreement with this position, based on their experience. They scored the role of advocate as "very important" in the cases of one-third of the 120 children in their care. Most often cited was the need to intervene on behalf of a child in school.

Collective bargainers. During the past year, a few parents in the project have introduced the idea of organizing a collective approach to deal with school-related problems. They want to create a structure through which they might negotiate with the school authorities. In short, they are interested in collective bargaining; they want to establish some base of organized power through which they may work out their grievances and problems.

During the spring of 1967, the staff helped the project parents mount a demonstration in front of the central office of the New York City Board of Education. The protest was over the board's resistance to their local school board's selection of a district superintendent.[6] The logic supporting such a strategy is clear. As Carlin *et al.* indicate:

> Because of their powerless position, often the most effective remedies for the poor are those which allow a *collective* challenge of the status quo to combat institutionalized abuses which no single individual could effectively call into question. Thus, in the struggle for civil rights the mass demonstration has been an important tool for rallying public support and for welding the Negroes themselves into a politically effective movement.[7]

STRUCTURAL PROBLEM

Events of the kind mentioned previously have involved the project's staff in a variety of activities that were not anticipated at the outset of the program in 1965. The program initially defined dropping out mainly in terms of the individual child's personal or family-related problems. However, experience has indicated that the core issue in the dropout process is often structural. That is, while the individual student, and frequently his family, may display troublesome behavior (as defined by school authorities), the behavior itself is often rooted in the very definition the school makes of the ongoing social relationship between the school as a system and the individual child and his family. For example, the school may expect the parent of a child in trouble to come to the school to discuss the problem. The ghetto parent, on the other hand, may be fearful or timid about such a meeting for a number of complex reasons. If the school authorities interpret this as a lack of parental interest and responsibility and if no effective com-

---

[3] *See* Charles F. Grosser, "Community Development Programs Serving the Urban Poor," *Social Work,* Vol. 10, No. 3 (July 1965), pp. 15–21; and Richard A. Cloward and Frances Fox Piven, "The Weapon of Poverty: Birth of a Movement," *The Nation,* Vol. 204, No. 19 (May 8, 1967), pp. 582–588.

[4] *See* Scott Briar, "The Casework Predicament," *Social Work,* Vol. 13, No. 1 (January 1968), pp. 5–11, and other articles addressing this theme in "Social Casework: Past, Present, and Future," a series of articles in the same issue dedicated to the late Gordon Hamilton.

[5] For a discussion of the ruling, *see* "Suspension from School," *New York Times,* April 11, 1967, p. 38.

[6] The local school board is a basic administrative unit of the New York City school system and the district superintendent is its chief officer.

[7] Jerome E. Carlin, Jan Howard, and Sheldon L. Messinger, "Civil Justice and the Poor: Issues for Sociological Research," *Law and Society Review,* Vol. 1, No. 1 (November 1966), p. 27.

munication is ever achieved between the school and parent, the process of leaving school early may be advanced for that child.

On this point, which is crucial for understanding the structural view being described here, the way parents may be defined as deviant by school personnel is a two-step affair: (1) The parents do not live up to the school's middle-class expectations. They are believed not to care about their children enough to come to the school to discuss a problem. (2) The parents, having demonstrated this dereliction of parental duty, do not need, the school feels, to be regarded as fully responsible and respectable members of society. They and their children are thus relegated to an inferior status in the eyes of school officials.

Such failure to perform serves to confirm for the school the more basic low status of all poor persons in this society. As Coser indicates: "What *is* sociologically relevant is poverty as a socially recognized condition, as a social status." [8] Poor people are expected to live under different rules from those that apply to more fortunate citizens. In its relationship to the institutional structure, the poor status is akin to that of the outcast because poor persons are in many ways outside the structure. Not only with respect to education, but also with regard to every major social institution, the poor find themselves set apart, treated differentially, and defined by another set of rules.[9]

It is on the basis of this structural estrangement that the project staff find themselves in roles that involve working toward structural rearrangements. As mediators, interpreters, convenors, advocates, and supporters of collective action, they function to connect their estranged and politically deprived clients with the official decision-makers. Thus, in addition to counseling, remediation, or, in some cases, therapy, the staff has found it necessary to address structural issues that occur again and again in the life situations of the project's children and parents.

Seen from this perspective, the school dropout who is a member of an economically and socially deprived group may be someone who was never a part of the system. The final severing of relations represented by dropping out of school may thus be seen as the cessation of a struggle to enter a relatively closed system with strict prerequisites for effective participation, rather than only a calculated decision to resign membership.

It should be evident that the work roles required to intervene effectively in the problem of school dropouts are complex. These roles transcend those traditionally associated with social casework and group work practice. One question raised by this role complexity is the way in which the roles should be allocated for maximum program efficiency. The experience of the demonstration project described here suggests that, with adequate training and a reasonable work load, one versatile worker could handle many of the roles associated with the complex problem-solving process. Thus, as the need required, he could function as counselor, advocate, interpreter, mediator, and family caseworker. On the other hand, the management of collective action might require a more specialized worker—a community organizer. The reason for this becomes evident when one considers not only the kinds of skills required to support the organization of structures that deal with community issues but also the amount of time needed to see a given social action project through from initiation to conclusion.

A complete analysis of work roles requires a consideration of the organizational context within which such roles are carried out. Certainly, no social work role will

---

[8] Lewis A. Coser, "The Sociology of Poverty," *Social Problems*, Vol. 13, No. 2 (Fall 1965), p. 141.

[9] With regard to the double standard for the poor, *see* Carlin *et al., op. cit.;* Harold L. Solomon, "This New Fetish for Indigency: Justice and Poverty in an Affluent Society," *Columbia Law Review*, Vol. 66, No. 2 (1966), pp. 248–274; and Lawrence M. Friedman, "Public Housing and the Poor: An Overview," *California Law Review*, Vol. 54, No. 2 (May 1966), pp. 642–669.

4

be executed with maximum efficiency without strong agency support and direction. The organizational integration of worker role and agency structure will now be considered in terms of six interrelated factors that are presumed to shape an agency's program: (1) the scope of the agency's activities, (2) the theoretical input that articulates agency policy, (3) the value orientation that influences agency decision-making, (4) the relationship of the agency to its clientele, (5) the nature and source of the agency's power as an urban social institution, and (6) the relationship between the agency and its workers.

SCOPE OF AGENCY'S ACTIVITIES

The field of action an agency defines as its domain has an obvious relationship to the kind of roles agency workers will be expected to play. For example, an agency that is mainly concerned with mental health and individual rehabilitation will require a role of therapist. An agency involved in legal aid will require a role of advocate. A community center usually has a variety of concerns revolving around the well-being of an entire neighborhood and its residents. This diversification of activities virtually dictates a complex and varied set of work roles for agency personnel, through either a complex role set in terms of individual workers or an organizational division of labor or both. The diverse work roles required for an adequate stay-in-school program, as described in this paper, would seem to be most appropriately carried out within the framework of a program that was broadly defined in terms of the agency's scope and purpose. The essential principle at work is that the range of the agency's actions will define the final limits of the work roles its staff may effectively perform.

THEORETICAL INPUT

For a social welfare program to maintain a rational continuity, it must be based on some theory—sometimes explicit, often implicit—of human behavior. Other things being equal, the more adequate and explicit the theory, the more rational and systematic will be the agency's judgment in terms of its policy and program.

Although a broadly focused agency requires the utilization of a variety of social and psychological theories at the service level, two general theoretical viewpoints may be considered to be most significant in terms of the present discussion. They are the order theory and the conflict theory of human societies. Since the main concern of order theorists is to explain the stability of society, they are apt to view social conflict as dysfunctional; since the interests of the conflict theorists are mainly in the direction of explaining social change, they are apt to view a rigid social order as dysfunctional. This difference is, of course, a matter of emphasis rather than of kind. As many social theorists have suggested, both viewpoints are indispensable to a comprehensive understanding of social behavior. Although the integration of these viewpoints is held to be a theoretical impossibility by some, Coser suggests:

> It seems high time finally to realize that whenever we deal with temporary equilibria it behooves us to investigate the peculiar conflicting forces that led to their establishment in the first place. Conversely, we must be sensitized to the fact that wherever there is conflict or disruption there will be social forces that press toward the establishment of some new kind of equilibrium.[10]

An awareness of both theoretical viewpoints would seem to be essential if social welfare agencies hope to influence processes that will lead toward improved social conditions in complex American communities. As was suggested earlier, the need for structural change to alleviate the powerlessness of the poor would not be perceived by an agency whose leadership was unaware both of the nature of institutions that function to maintain the status

---

[10] Lewis A. Coser, *Continuities in the Study of Social Conflict* (New York: Free Press, 1967), p. 10.

quo and of the kinds of forces that must be developed in order to achieve structural change.

The social welfare agency's comprehension of these theories and the utilization of them in policy-making would seem to increase the possibility of what Ohlin has called the need to represent "indigenous interests" as opposed to those of the more established dominant community.[11] Certain questions then arise: How is the problem of the agency's allegiance to be resolved? For whom does the agency really speak? On what basis, financial or otherwise, does the agency maintain its integrity as a mediator of or participant in community conflict? As Marris and Rein point out repeatedly, the answer is by no means clear. It is suggested that the articulation of the two theoretical viewpoints of human relationships facilitates a recognition of the dilemma and balance needed to reduce ambiguity and its consequences.[12]

VALUE ORIENTATION

It is well known that there is often a strong association between theory and value orientation in an action program. For example, Saul Alinsky's overriding emphasis is on the functions of conflict to achieve meaningful social change on behalf of the poor.

In one family life program, the consensus at a recent staff meeting was that perhaps more than 90 percent of the agency's clients were mentally ill.[13] This judgment is entirely understandable, given the predominantly psychoanalytic orientation of the agency's staff and leadership. For example, when the staff was asked to describe the kinds of behavior that led them to judge that a family or individual required therapeutic treatment, responses were often as follows: "absence of motivation, practicality, gratitude, or desire to be helped; resistance to accepting the need to change patterns of behavior; lack of ambition; and unwillingness to follow bureaucratic regulations." In this case, the agency's orientation is transparently clear. Lower-class clients' unwillingness to move quickly in the direction of adopting middle-class values is interpreted by the staff to mean that such clients suffer from some form of mental illness.

In an effort to get poor people to adopt middle-class values, an agency is apt to try short-circuiting the historical stages involved in the assimilation process by emphasizing resocialization and therapeutic relationships as the most appropriate modes of programming rather than collective bargaining and the building of institutionalized power among the disadvantaged. Pressing the value of equality of opportunity is apt to reinforce the caretaker viewpoint since equality does not usually work out in terms of collective opportunity but rather individual opportunity. Thus, a disadvantaged collectivity's need for structural change is ignored when the staff focuses its attention on individualized rehabilitation or assimilation. Certainly, any agency that predicates programming tightly on the basis of individualized treatment will not often allow its workers to diversify their work roles in the direction of the political stance represented by advocacy and collective action.

AGENCY-CLIENT RELATIONSHIP

Agencies with long traditions of caretaking are not apt to be accepted by local activists when support is required for conflict-oriented programming. If the agency is perceived as being allied to the status quo, it will be difficult to convince its clientele

---

[11] Lloyd Ohlin, "Issues in the Development of Indigenous Social Movements Among Residents of Deprived Urban Areas" (October 1960), p. 17. (Mimeographed.)

[12] Peter Marris and Martin Rein, *Dilemmas of Social Reform: Poverty and Community Action in the United States* (New York: Atherton Press, 1967), pp. 164–190.

[13] The agency used as an example here functions to assist migrant Puerto Rican families to settle and assimilate into an eastern metropolitan community.

that it can actually become partisan on their behalf. Nor are disadvantaged clients likely to be inclined to accept a thoroughly middle-class oriented agency as a mediator to settle community issues.

The trust required for an agency to function effectively as an advocate and organizer of its disadvantaged clients is best developed through consistent demonstration in its actions of its commitment—even positive bias—to the clients' needs. In other words, to be accepted by the disadvantaged, the agency must demonstrate that it is with its people, will not let them be abused, and will fight to win in their name. This does not imply that the agency must be against everyone else. In most cases of social conflict the outcome is not a win-or-lose situation. Both parties may often be able to gain something; an exchange of rewards and concessions is a continual possibility. But it goes without saying that the agency must mediate conflict without selling out. The case is not too dissimilar from that of the mediator in collective bargaining in union-management relations.

The agency's clients will consider the worker—as an agency representative—according to their image of the agency. If they think the agency is satisfactory, the worker will generally be accepted; if the agency is defined as unacceptable, so too are its representatives. The lines delimiting the extent of acceptability are often clearly drawn. The welfare client is not apt to look on the welfare department worker with much favor. The parole officer is not likely to have the full confidence of his parolees. On the other hand, workers from an agency with a history of activism will not usually be looked on as caretakers by their clients.

AGENCY POWER

An agency must gauge the extent of its power in relation to those whom it wishes to bring to the bargaining table, especially when dealing with social conflict. Even with individual advocacy, the relative power of the agency is significant. An agency committed to the disadvantaged, which has withstood the test of battle in relationships with significant political or economic institutions, has a solid basis for future social action. If it has proved weak or ineffective, the agency is not apt to transmit confidence either to its staff or its clientele. It is certainly not likely to command the respect of its opponents. An agency that has been co-opted by a strong, conservative institution may seem to have power, but its power is not its own, since the agency lacks the necessary autonomy to make its own choices.

In any case, power is seldom absolute. What is essential for the proper representation of a disadvantaged clientele in bargaining is being resourceful, resilient, and at times simply *guapo* (tough), on the model of a well-organized labor union. A competing party does not come to the bargaining table out of goodness or a sense of fair play, but rather because he is reasonably certain that he will lose something by not doing so. The staff member's advocacy on behalf of disadvantaged clients will be effective to the extent that the adversary realizes the worker represents and can deliver agency influence, resources, and, if called for, institutionalized power.

AGENCY-WORKER RELATIONSHIP

The need for clarity of the agency's policy about the worker's function requires specific emphasis. The worker must know just what roles he is expected to play, when to play them, and just how far he can push. In other words, he must understand the agency's expectations and the field of social action within which he will operate. Furthermore, he must be able to work out his conception of his role with his supervisor, so that a gap between the agency's expectation and his personal conception does not emerge (or if it does, the reasons for the discrepancy may be examined). Furthermore, if the two are relatively congruent,

7

performance can be evaluated in a framework of mutual expectations.

CONCLUSIONS

Several interrelated principles that deserve special emphasis emerge from this discussion of new professional work roles and their integration into agency structure. They are as follows:

1. During the past few years the context within which American society has dealt and continues to deal with the problems of poverty and various forms of social deviance has changed swiftly and radically. A variety of highly polarized, large-scale conflict situations have led the society to re-examine its position vis-à-vis its own outcasts. The War on Poverty, in its own erratic and blind way, symbolized the early innovative spirit of the decade. Recently, widespread dissent and collective violence have advanced as social movements. Under these conditions, innovation in social work is occurring and will continue to occur in massive proportions in both public and private social welfare and should be welcomed.

2. The course of innovation will lead to strains within social welfare agencies and between agencies and their various publics. The changing nature of the professional social work role inevitably will lead to the problem of agency adjustment to the demands of new developments. Agency decision-makers will be challenged to lead their organizations through the maze of often-conflicting currents in American social thought and provide their workers with an agency policy, structure, and set of specific work roles that will remain abreast of the times and meet changing definitions of clients' needs.[14]

14 For a further discussion of this point, *see* Sydney E. Bernard, Emeric Kurtagh, and Harold R. Johnson, "The Neighborhood Service Organization: Specialist in Social Welfare Innovation," *Social Work,* Vol. 13, No. 1 (January 1968), pp. 76–84.

3. Social workers are likely to find that they will increasingly be confronted by the need to act as bridges between politically motivated, disadvantaged, and alienated groups and the dominant society, which is often hostile and angry toward both social workers and their clients. The demands required by this role will make it necessary for them to have new knowledge of and empathy with the variety of systems with which they must deal. They must also have the ability to handle effectively social conflict as both a problem and a technique of change, a general willingness to participate in public debate on highly controversial issues, and a capacity to deal with complicated social structures and processes. All these work-role modifications must be added to the social worker's long-standing capacity to deal effectively with personality stress and intrafamilial strain.

4. As work roles for social workers become more complex, the strategy of role allocation and the need for a division of labor, as well as the kinds of professional preparation required to play emerging new work roles, will become significant problems for long-range planning by the profession. At best, modification of traditional practices and agency functions proceeds slowly. Both involve the difficult task of learning to intervene effectively with respect to widespread institutional strain. Both obviously need to be supported by dramatic and often difficult shifts in the content of graduate professional training. The danger is that the fields of practice and professional education will become grossly misaligned. An even greater danger, not likely to occur, is that both will become anachronistic in a rapidly changing society in which poverty and social deviance no longer mean what they once meant and charity and rehabilitation are no longer accepted as adequate substitutes for social change and social justice.

NASW REPRINTS

Mental health workers are critically examining modes of service delivery. Crisis intervention offers a way to apply to mental health problems some concepts of primary prevention that have been successful in the public health field.

Crisis intervention: theory in search of a program

by Richard A. Pasewark and Dale A. Albers

Richard A. Pasewark, Ph.D., is Professor of Psychology and Director of Clinical Training, University of Wyoming, Laramie, Wyoming. Dale Albers, DSW, is Associate Professor, Department of Sociology, University of South Dakota, Vermillion, South Dakota.

Tremendous strides have been made in the field of public health in recent decades. Many former scourges, threatening young or old or both, have been drastically cut down or even practically eliminated—such as tuberculosis, polio, malaria, and typhoid fever. The mental health field cannot point proudly to similar dramatic advances.

Can some of the same concepts and basic techniques that have proved successful in public health be applied effectively on a wide scale to the field of mental health? The authors believe that this can be done through crisis intervention.

Crisis intervention has been developing over a number of years. Workers using the crisis approach have reported many instances of success in dealing with problems arising from specific situations and events such as illegitimacy, pregnancy and birth, suicide and other deaths, and poverty.[1] However, there is a notable absence of programs either totally or primarily oriented to this approach.

To substantiate the viewpoint that general application of crisis intervention can revitalize the mental health field and offer hope for successful primary prevention of mental disorders, an explanation is presented of what crisis theory is, how it developed, and how it might be applied broadly to mental health and the helping services.

The development of crisis intervention theory owes much to Erikson, Lindemann, and Caplan—all associated with Harvard University or the Harvard Medical School. They evolved three cornerstones of the theory: the concept of developmental crises, redefinition of transient personality disorders as life crises having a predictable pattern, and application of the public health model to mental health.

Erikson contributed the idea that in nor-

[1] *See* Karen A. Signell, "The Crisis of Unwed Motherhood: A Consultation Approach," *Community Mental Health Journal*, Vol. 5, No. 4 (August 1969), pp. 304–313; Gerald Caplan, "Mental Hygiene Work with Expectant Mothers," *Mental Hygiene*, Vol. 35, No. 1 (January 1951), pp. 41–50; Gerald Caplan, Edward A. Mason, and David M. Kaplan, "Four Studies of Crisis in Parents of Prematures," *Community Mental Health Journal*, Vol.

Reprinted from SOCIAL WORK, 17 (March 1972), pp. 70–77. Copyright © by the National Association of Social Workers, Inc., 1972.

CAO–008–C

mal growth the individual experiences several specific developmental crises that he must surmount if he is to become a mature, integrated adult. He defined crisis as "a necessary turning point, a crucial moment, when development must move one way or another, marshaling resources of growth, recovery, and further differentiation."[2] He identified eight such types of developmental crises occurring during the normal span of life from infancy through childhood, adolescence, and maturity, to old age and senescence.

Lindemann's interest focused on transient personality disorders—precipitated by unusual environmental stress. The assumption is that removing stress will ameliorate or eliminate the observed behavioral symptoms. Lindemann was especially concerned with grief reactions following a loved one's death and concluded that an individual had to make an adjustment to the crisis such a death precipitated. His investigations contributed to crisis theory the idea that reactions to crisis follow a predictable pattern and have specific, identifiable stages.[3]

Caplan was a forceful advocate of crisis intervention theory. A major thrust of his work was toward applying public health principles to community mental health problems. Specifically, Caplan was concerned with primary, secondary, and tertiary prevention and ways to apply these public health concepts to mental health activities.[4]

Primary prevention aims to reduce the incidence of a disorder by altering the environment so that it restrains the disease process or by making the individual less susceptible. Secondary prevention tries to keep a mild disorder from becoming a severe one. Early case-finding and treatment are stressed. Tertiary prevention aims to keep a serious disorder from producing permanent disability. All three endeavor to prevent any individual from being a source of contagion.

In essence, a crisis might be considered analogous to a learning dilemma. In both the person experiences a new situation or event for which he has no adequate coping behaviors. The strategy in crisis intervention is to provide the individual with appropriate behavioral patterns that will enable him to deal effectively with the specific crisis. Crisis theorists have not delineated the mode of intervention; one assumes that the techniques to be used remain the prerogative of the intervenor.

A number of overt or tacit assumptions are made in crisis theory, such as:

Crisis is not a pathological experience. Acute symptoms manifested in crisis do not necessarily indicate previous personality disturbance or reflect current pathology. Instead they mirror first a dearth of available mechanisms for dealing with the situation, then groping behavior that seeks to resolve it effectively, and eventually the behavior adopted for coping with the crisis. The basic optimism of the theory is seen in the point of view that a person's troubled behavior in a crisis may reflect struggle with a current problem rather than past or present deviation from the normal. In some ways, this assumption is reminiscent of Jung's view of psychiatric disturbance as symptomatic of the organism's dissatisfaction with a current developmental state and of the flux in personality as it attempts to deal with the situation.[5]

1, No. 2 (Summer 1965), pp. 149–161; Edwin S. Shneidman and Norman L. Farberow, "The Los Angeles Suicide Prevention Center: A Demonstration of Public Health Feasibilities," *American Journal of Public Health,* Vol. 55, No. 1 (January 1965), pp. 21–26; Erich Lindemann, "Symptomatology and Management of Acute Grief," *American Journal of Psychiatry,* Vol. 101, No. 2 (September 1944), pp. 141–148; Erich Lindemann, Warren Vaughn, and Manon McGinnis, "Preventive Intervention in a Four Year Old Child Whose Father Committed Suicide," in Caplan, ed., *Emotional Problems of Early Childhood* (New York: Basic Books, 1955), pp. 5–30; and Harris B. Peck, Seymour R. Kaplan, and Melvin Roman, "Prevention, Treatment, and Social Action: A Strategy of Intervention in a Disadvantaged Urban Area," *American Journal of Orthopsychiatry,* Vol. 36, No. 1 (January 1966), pp. 57–69.

[2] Erik H. Erikson, *Identity: Youth and Crisis* (New York: W. W. Norton & Co., 1968), p. 16.

[3] Op. cit.

[4] Gerald Caplan, *Principles of Preventive Psychiatry* (New York: Basic Books, 1964), pp. 35–127.

2

Crises are temporary and therefore self-limiting. All crises must come to an end; none continues indefinitely. Some adjustment is made to the event be it adequate or inadequate. It is assumed that different categories of crises have different temporal histories. For example, the crisis precipitated by the death of a loved one differs in length from that caused by the incarceration of a spouse or son.

Each type of crisis pursues a course made up of typical, identifiable stages. Crisis behaviors and reaction patterns can be anticipated. Further, each crisis category has an individualized progression that is theoretically discrete from that of all others. For example, Lindemann distinguished the following successive stages in grief and bereavement: (1) disbelief, (2) denial, (3) symptoms of grief or bereavement that include (a) somatic distress, (b) preoccupation with images of the deceased, (c) guilt, (d) hostility toward the deceased and others such as physicians, nurses, and friends, and (e) loss of typical patterns of conduct and emergence of such behaviors as withdrawal, lack of initiative, and dependence, (4) emancipation from bondage to the deceased, (5) readjustment to an environment in which the deceased is missing, and (6) formation of new interpersonal relationships and behavior patterns.[6] It is normal for a person to experience each stage of crisis. In fact, omission of any stage in the progression suggests that he may not be coping adequately with the crisis.

The individual in crisis is especially amenable to help. Crisis is a critical period during which the individual actively seeks new resources and activities. He is therefore prone to accept help and to learn and incorporate new behaviors.

A small amount of assistance makes it possible for a person to surmount a crisis. This assumption holds that only limited resources and assistance must be expended

> **". . . there is no conclusive evidence that . . . promising results will in fact be realized if the crisis model is generally adopted."**

in the intervention process. Old defenses are weakened and resistance to the development of new behaviors is diminished.

Weathering a current crisis permits the individual to cope more effectively with future crises. This is probably the most important assumption made in crisis theory. Problem-solving behaviors learned in the immediate situation can be applied effectively to subsequently encountered crises. It may be presumed that inadequate reactions can make future adjustments to new crises less effective.

Various workers in crisis theory have categorized the different types of crises that can be experienced. Caplan, Hill, and Eliot have probably evolved the most meaningful classification systems.

Caplan identifies two categories.[7] The first group includes crises precipitated by changes in the everyday course of living—such as entry into school, birth of a sibling, emergence of heterosexual interests, marriage, birth of a child, retirement, and death. The second category includes crises occasioned by unusually hazardous events—such as acute or chronic illness, accidents, or family dislocations—which might occur to an individual, a member of his immediate or extended family, or a close associate.

Hill also names two categories, but places greater stress on the family as the focus of crisis.[8] His first group includes crises precipitated by extrafamilial events, such as war, flood, economic depression, or religious persecution. Crises in his second

5 Carl G. Jung, "Two Essays on Analytical Psychology," in Herbert Read, Michael Fordham, and Gerhard Adler, eds., *The Collected Works of C. G. Jung*, Vol. 7 (New York: Pantheon Books, 1966), p. 10.

6 Lindemann, op. cit.
7 *Principles of Preventive Psychiatry*, pp. 34–55.
8 Reuben Hill, "Generic Features of Families Under Stress," *Social Casework*, Vol. 39, Nos. 2–3 (February–March 1958), pp. 139–150.

category are precipitated by intrafamilial events or situations, such as desertion, alcoholism, or infidelity. Hill believes that extrafamilial crises tend to solidify the family and enhance its crisis-meeting resources but that intrafamilial crises typically lead to its demoralization.

Eliot lists four categories also built around the family unit.[9] In the first, crises of "dismemberment," loss of a family member is experienced either through death or from extended separation because of war, imprisonment, employment dislocation, or hospitalization for physical or mental disorders.

His second category, crises of "ascension," involves an unplanned addition to the family unit. Examples are an unwanted pregnancy, an illegitimate birth, the return of a deserting father, or the unwanted addition of a stepsibling, a stepparent, or an aged parent.

In Eliot's third category, crises of demoralization, the family unit remains the same size, but one of its members experiences an undesirable event or condition. These crises include a husband's or father's nonsupport, infidelity, alcoholism, drug addiction, delinquency, unemployment, vocational demotion, or mental disorder. Eliot's fourth class embraces crises of demoralization accompanied by either dismemberment or ascension (loss or addition of a family member). Examples are a runaway adolescent, a father's desertion, divorce, imprisonment, suicide, homicide, or institutionalization for a mental disorder.

STAGES OF CRISIS

In the sequence of interactions leading up to the state of perceived crisis, an objective event first takes place, such as the death of a loved one, unemployment of the breadwinner, or birth of a child.[10] The event then interacts with the individual's or group's crisis-meeting resources, which may be excellent, adequate, poor, or nonexistent. From this interaction, a definition of the event is made. The same event might be defined similarly or quite differently by different individuals or families. For instance, because of varying crisis-meeting resources and extenuating circumstances, a breadwinner's sudden unemployment might be defined as a severe, moderate, or mild crisis or even as no crisis at all.

If defining the event leads to a perception of crisis, then a period of disorganization inevitably follows. This is characterized by various maladaptive behaviors or psychiatric syndromes such as grief, withdrawal, inactivity, or heightened anxiety. There is exaggerated use of currently available defense systems and behaviors that are not suited to the crisis situation. Because the individual is experiencing difficulty in his groping and problem-solving behavior, he tends to be more receptive to outside assistance and resources during this period.

The period of disorganization is followed by a period of reorganization, which has clearly identifiable phases. In the initial phase of correct cognitive perception, the problem is maintained at a conscious level. For example, in the case of death the individual recognizes that feelings of dependency and support can no longer be anchored to the deceased. During the next phase, management of affect through awareness of feelings, there is an appropriate acceptance and release of feelings associated with the crisis. After the death of a loved one, emotions such as remorse, guilt, and hostility are accepted and find suitable expression.

The last phase is the development of patterns for seeking and using help. The individual begins to adopt constructive means for dealing with the problem and uses other persons and organizations to help him in this task. For example, the widow may use the state employment agency to find a job or, encouraged by a friend, she may

[9] T. D. Eliot, "Handling Family Strains and Shocks," in Howard Becker and Reuben Hill, eds., *Family, Marriage, and Parenthood* (Boston: D. C. Heath & Co., 1955), pp. 616–641.

[10] The following description of the stages of crisis is derived from the work of Hill, op. cit.; and Lydia Rapoport, "The State of Crisis: Some Theoretical Considerations," *Social Service Review*, Vol. 36, No. 2 (June 1962), pp. 212–213.

4

> *"Increasing the experience with crises might also be an educative task. Efforts would be directed toward permitting individuals to experience 'sham' crises."*

become active in volunteer associations to fill the void created by her husband's death. At the end of this phase, habitual behavioral patterns have developed that allow flexible use of persons and external resources not only in crisis but in ordinary situations. Essentially, the individual's horizons and resources have expanded. In other words, the level of reorganization achieved after crisis is higher than the precrisis behavior level. However, this does not always occur. The reorganization level can be the same as, lower, or higher than the precrisis level.

Various writers have cataloged the following characteristics that seem to be associated with an individual's or a family's ability to cope successfully with crisis-producing events:[11] (1) behavioral adaptability and flexibility within the family, (2) affection among family members, (3) good marital adjustment between husband and wife, (4) companionable parent-child relations, (5) family members' participation in decision-making, (6) wife's participation in husband's social activities, (7) nonmarginal economic status, (8) individual's or family's direct or vicarious experience with the type of crisis encountered, (9) objective knowledge of facets of a specific crisis before it occurs—which presupposes the individual's or group's capacity to discuss openly feelings about events that might precipitate crisis, such as drug abuse or impending birth, marriage, or death—(10) established patterns of interaction with the extended family, neighbors, and friends.[12]

Two conclusions emerge from a study of this list. First, an individual needs and may even require other persons to surmount a crisis. These persons may be members of the immediate or extended family, friends, or social workers. Second, facilitating communication between the individual and these persons mitigates the severity of the crisis.

PRIMARY PREVENTION

The principles of crisis intervention, practically applied, have profound implications for mental health and the helping services. Crisis concepts seem particularly applicable to primary and secondary prevention efforts.

In primary prevention, the intervenor may direct his efforts chiefly toward eliminating or minimizing events capable of inducing crisis. Distinction should be made between different classes of events. There are some events that, with present knowledge, can be eliminated or minimized by appropriate social action. Unemployment and marginal economic circumstances might be practically abolished by vast social and economic reforms. The possibility of war might be greatly reduced by forming an international government invested with viable responsibility. Birth injuries, some forms of mental retardation, and certain types of illness leading to death might be prevented through expanded medical services. Birth of children can be prevented through contraception or abortion. Acci-

---

[11] See Caplan, *Principles of Preventive Psychiatry*, pp. 44–48; Hill, op. cit., p. 148; Rapoport, op. cit., p. 216; Jay L. Rooney, "Special Stress on Low-Income Families," *Social Casework*, Vol. 39, Nos. 2–3 (February–March, 1958), pp. 150–158.

[12] Individuals and families best able to surmount the crisis of separation in Great Britain during World War II frequently mentioned friends, neighbors, and relatives who provided assistance. Much to the chagrin of the helping professions, these families rarely mentioned that the church, physicians, or social agencies played a significant role in their adjustment. See Hill, op. cit., p. 148.

5

dent control might reduce accidental deaths. Premarital counseling might prevent certain divorces. Increased use of community facilities and homebound programs for the mentally ill could minimize family separations occurring from hospitalization.

Knowledge is currently lacking about ways to prevent or minimize certain events. Among these would be death resulting from certain disease processes and aging, hospitalization for various forms of physical and mental illness, and many divorces. Optimistically, increased knowledge should extend life and promote health and marital well-being so that most of these events should eventually be classified in the first category.

There are also events that cannot be prevented, including those that people would not wish to prevent even if they could. Among these are the broad developmental crises experienced in life, such as birth, adolescence, marriage, and retirement.

Effective primary prevention measures, besides influencing events, may strengthen the individual's or group's crisis-meeting resources. The intervenor's efforts would be directed toward developing patterns of interpersonal relations that aim to increase family members' communcation, individual and group experience with crises, and accessibility to social resources at appropriate crisis points.

Increasing communication within family units might prove to be essentially educational. Procedures used could include premarital, marital, and ongoing educative group counseling and discussions emphasizing the necessity of familial communication, ways to maintain it, and ways to avoid communication breakdown.

Increasing the experience with crises might also be an educative task. Efforts would be directed toward permitting individuals to experience "sham" crises. To a greater degree than at present, the helping professions would be concerned with preparing premarital groups, groups of expectant parents, and drug groups to handle experiences likely to be encountered. These programs would focus not only on presenting factual information about the event but also on dealing with the resultant crisis. Thus the focus of a drug group would not be limited to incidence rates, laws, and physiological effects related to drugs. The group would also discuss anticipated personal and familial crises, such as that which might occur when a mother discovers a "joint" in her son's jacket pocket. They would "experience" these crises also through such techniques as role-playing, psychodrama, and sensitivity sessions. Similar programs might be developed on mental disorders, retirement, death, and many other topics. These mock experiences would be somewhat comparable to the childhood fantasies that Erikson regards as valuable preparation for future roles.[13]

To make social resources more readily accessible to individuals in crisis, two approaches seem feasible. First, currently available personnel and services might be brought closer. To accomplish this, the helping professions would have to assume a more active stance than at present. Rather than passively waiting for the client experiencing crisis to be referred or voluntarily come to the social work agency, manpower resources would be deployed to locales in which crises were most likely to occur. For example, rather than establishing a network of mental health centers, mental health personnel would be located in potential crisis sites, such as day care centers, schools, obstetrical wards, and community centers in slum areas. A second complementary approach would be to identify crisis-prone individuals and then mobilize resources to provide them with readily accessible services. In this area, development of "risk registers" might be fruitful. Thus a crisis-prone pregnant woman would, on reporting to her physician, find a group of persons ready to assist her in pregnancy—the alerted physician himself, the pediatrician who would eventually care for her newborn child, the public health nurse who could provide pre- and postnatal care, per-

[13] Erik H. Erikson, *Insight and Responsibility* (New York: W. W. Norton & Co., 1964), pp. 120–121.

> *"Individuals experiencing crisis often have no previous knowledge of, let alone contacts with, agencies providing assistance."*

haps even a mental health worker to involve her in group discussions, and a housekeeper aide to assist her during the difficult early postnatal months. If the intervenor can affect either the event or the individual's crisis resources, the event's definition and the nature of the perceived crisis will be altered considerably.

SECONDARY PREVENTION

Applying crisis theory to secondary prevention is basically dealing with the intervenor's role when an event is already experienced as a crisis. The efforts that might be taken roughly parallel the phases in the period of reorganization.

Establishing or facilitating communication. In crisis situations communication between family members is often lacking or blocked. For example, a family's discovery that a son or daughter is to be the parent of an illegitimate child or is a drug-user frequently causes abrupt cessation of communication between family members and the offender. In such cases, professional skills and resources might well be most efficaciously used to try to restore disrupted family communication and initiate contacts with community agencies potentially able to assist in the crisis.

Individuals experiencing crisis often have no previous knowledge of, let alone contacts with, agencies providing assistance. A case in point is that of parents who give birth to a retarded child. They may be unaware of the immediate help available through the National Association for Retarded Children and the crippled children's division of the local health depart-

ment. Nor are such parents necessarily aware of help obtainable later from state vocational rehabilitation agencies for training activities. Similarly, a woman of 40, suddenly widowed, may not know about such community resources as state unemployment or child welfare services. A paramount role of helping persons in time of crisis, and probably one of the more meaningful ones, would be to help the individual identify and get in touch with community social agencies most able to provide assistance.

Assisting the individual or family to perceive the event correctly and to understand it. Cases in point would be the parents of a youth apprehended for possession of marijuana and the parents whose unmarried daughter tells them she is pregnant. In the former instance, the intervenor might help the parents recognize the conflict between law and reality in drug use and understand other "reality-myth" distinctions concerning drug use and abuse. In the latter instance, the intervenor could explain the effects of the birth on the daughter and the family and present various alternatives for dealing with the situation.

Assisting the individual or family to manage emotions and feelings, keep affects conscious, and deal with them openly. In the cases of the drug offender and the unmarried mother, the intervenor might best serve by helping those involved to recognize and express feelings of shame and to realize how this emotion is related to their hostile reactions. The intervenor might also provide appropriate means for releasing these sentiments in discussion.

CONCLUSIONS

At the time when mental health workers are critically reexamining modes of service delivery, the application of crisis theory principles to mental health seems especially worthy of attention. More than most approaches and models, it offers a consistent view of mental health problems and suggests guidelines for the direction and thrust of mental health efforts. Essentially, it advocates an active and preventive stance— eliminating specific events associated with crisis, enhancing crisis-meeting resources before crisis is experienced, and intervening actively in crisis before maladaptive problem-solving patterns develop.

There are a number of reasons, however, why the crisis approach has not been widely adopted in the mental health field. First, it seems reasonable to suppose that a much greater commitment in finances and personnel would be required to implement crisis theory principles than is now made in mental health efforts. Current efforts, lip service to the contrary, focus primarily on tertiary prevention endeavors.

Second, widespread adoption of the crisis approach is risky. Despite reported successes in various limited endeavors, there is no conclusive evidence that such promising results will in fact be realized if the crisis model is generally adopted and resources are directed to the primary prevention efforts it involves.

Third, implementing crisis principles would demand a rather abrupt adjustment by mental health workers. They would have to become much more aggressive. They would have to make active efforts to eliminate or minimize crisis-producing events by altering social situations. They would have to intervene in the social scene to increase the crisis-resistance resources of normal individuals before society or these individuals themselves realized the need of such assistance. They would have to seek out actively individuals at an early stage of personal disorganization. In many ways the mental health worker's role would become that of social architect. Considerable question exists within the field itself about whether such intervention is an appropriate function of the mental health technician and professional.[14] The lay public is as yet unaware of this potential role.

Fourth, adoption of crisis principles would also raise considerable question concerning the wisdom of the field's present investment in the community mental health center model. Crisis theory principles at least create doubt concerning the efficacy of the community mental health center model for deploying services, in fact create doubt about whether these centers offer the most appropriate and effective means of dealing with mental health problems. Thus crisis intervention, although it has much to offer, is still a theory in search of a program.

---

14 *See* Dale Albers and Richard A. Pasewark, "How New are the New Comprehensive Mental Health Centers," in Willard F. Richan, ed., *Human Services and Social Work Responsibility* (New York: National Association of Social Workers, 1969), pp. 148–155; H. Warren Dunham, "Community Psychiatry: The Newest Therapeutic Bandwagon," *Archives of General Psychiatry*, Vol. 12, No. 3 (March 1965), pp. 303–313; David M. Mechanic, "Community Psychiatry: Some Sociological Perspectives and Implications," in Leigh M. Roberts, Seymour L. Halleck, and Martin B. Loeb, eds., *Community Psychiatry* (Madison: University of Wisconsin Press, 1966), pp. 201–222; Richard A. Pasewark and Max W. Rardin, "Theoretical Models in Community Mental Health," *Mental Hygiene*, Vol. 55, No. 3 (July 1971), pp. 358–364.

8

BY LYDIA RAPOPORT

Working with Families in Crisis: An Exploration in Preventive Intervention

THIS PAPER DESCRIBES preventive intervention work done with families considered to be in a state of crisis because of the birth of a premature infant. The work was an exploratory phase of a larger project conducted at the Harvard School of Public Health Family Guidance Center,[1] which studied the reaction patterns and coping mechanisms of families in crisis. Identifications of patterns, both adaptive and maladaptive, could serve as indices for prediction of outcome and also as a guide to caretakers and helping professions for the deployment of resources and for focused intervention.

Two related frames of reference guided this work: that of prevention as formulated and utilized in the public health field, and that of crisis theory as formulated by mental health investigators and social psychiatrists.

Prevention, in the public health field, is conceived of as a continuum of activities to protect the health of the community. These activities are classified as (1) health promotion, (2) specific protection, (3) early diagnosis and treatment, including case-finding, (4) disability limitation, and (5) rehabilitation.[2] The first two categories are in the nature of primary prevention, that is to say, intervention before a problem is manifest. Early diagnosis and treatment are considered to be secondary prevention, while the last two categories are classified as tertiary prevention. In general, most public health activities are directed at designated groups in the community which are considered, on the basis of epidemiological study, to be populations at risk. In this study, prematurity was considered to be a hazardous circumstance which poses a threat to family equilibrium and is likely to precipitate a family into a state of crisis. Therefore these families were designated as a "population at risk" and became a target for efforts of preventive intervention. The aim was to prevent mentally unhealthy consequences of the crisis which could interfere with the development of a sound mother-child relationship.

Numerous investigators have contributed to concepts of crisis, particularly Dr. Erich Lindemann and Dr. Gerald Caplan, both of Harvard University. In their formulation, crisis refers to the *state of the reacting individual* who finds himself in a hazardous situation.[3] Crisis in its simplest terms is defined as "an upset in a steady state." [4]

LYDIA RAPOPORT, M.S.S., *is lecturer at the School of Social Welfare, University of California, Berkeley, California. The work described in this article was conducted in 1959–60 while the author was research associate at the Harvard School of Public Health. The paper is drawn from a longer version presented at the residence seminar, University of California School of Social Welfare Extension, in June 1961.*

[1] Under the direction of Dr. Gerald Caplan, associate professor of mental health and director of community mental health at the Harvard School of Public Health.

[2] Hugh R. Leavell and E. G. Clark, *Preventive Medicine for the Doctor in His Community* (New York: McGraw-Hill Book Company, 1958), pp. 21–29.

[3] Erich Lindemann and Gerald Caplan, "A Conceptual Framework for Preventive Psychiatry." Unpublished paper.

[4] Formulated by Gerald Caplan in seminars at the Harvard School of Public Health, 1959–60.

There are many hazardous events or circumstances in the life cycle of an individual or family which threaten or upset the balance that has been achieved in the system of need-satisfaction and in the performance of social roles. Certain hazardous events, such as loss of a loved person, have an almost universal impact and would precipitate a state of crisis of varying intensity and duration in nearly all individuals.

UNDERLYING ASSUMPTIONS

It is postulated that in a state of crisis the habitual problem-solving activities are not adequate for a rapid re-establishment of equilibrium. The hazardous event that precipitates the crisis is of such a nature as to require a solution that is new to the individual in relation to his previous life experience. Many individuals are able to develop novel solutions out of their normal range of problem-solving mechanisms and can deal adequately with the hazardous event. Others are unable to respond with appropriate solutions, so that the hazardous event and its sequelae continue to be a source of stress that creates considerable maladaptation.

The hazardous event creates for the individual a problem in his current life situation. The problem can be conceived as either a threat, a loss, or a challenge. A threat may be directed to instinctual needs, or to the sense of integrity. A loss may be experienced as a state of acute deprivation. Furthermore, for each of these states there is a characteristic mode by which the ego tends to respond. Thus, a threat to need or integrity is responded to with anxiety. Loss or deprivation is responded to with depression. If the problem is viewed as a challenge it may be met with appropriate anxiety, fortified by hope and expectation of mastery. This, then, is more apt to lead to a mobilization of energy and to purposive problem-solving activities. In summary it may be said that there are three sets of interrelated factors which can produce a state of crisis: (1) a hazardous event which poses some threat; (2) a threat to instinctual need which is linked symbolically to earlier threats that have resulted in vulnerability or conflict in the personality; (3) inability to respond with adequate coping mechanisms.[5]

There are certain characteristics of the state of crisis. First, the period of crisis is time-limited—that is, the individual or family does manage, in due time, to achieve some solution for the problem. The crisis is resolved and a state of equilibrium is once again achieved. However, the outcome varies. Thus the new state of equilibrium may be the same, worse, or even better, from a mental health point of view, than that achieved prior to the crisis.

The second characteristic of the crisis state refers to phases that occur during the period of upset: first, there is a period of heightened tension; second, there is an attempt to solve the problem with habitual problem-solving mechanisms; third, emergency problem-solving mechanisms may be called on. The outcome may once again be variable: the problem may actually be solved, or the goals may be altered in order to achieve need-satisfaction and greater stability, or there may be a renunciation of desired goals.

The third—and for the practitioner the most important—characteristic is the fact that people are more susceptible to influence during a state of crisis. Moreover, the amount of activity on the part of helping persons does not have to be extensive. A little help, rationally directed and purposefully focused at a strategic time, is more effective than more extensive help given at a time of lesser emotional accessibility.

The outcome of a crisis is determined by numerous variables. Favorable environmental factors and current adaptive capacity are important. Less important in in-

5 Howard J. Parad and Gerald Caplan, "A Framework for Studying Families in Crisis," *Social Work*, Vol. 5, No. 3 (July 1960), p. 5.

fluencing outcome is the nature of the prior personality or psychopathology.[6] Most important of all is the accomplishment of, or failure to accomplish, certain specific psychological tasks and certain related problem-solving activities.

The mother who gives birth to a premature baby has to master certain specific psychological tasks and engage in certain problem-solving activities. These have been described as follows: [7]

Phase 1. Mother and infant are in the hospital after delivery. During this critical period the mother is faced with the following psychological tasks: She has to acknowledge that the infant's life is threatened and that survival in the early postnatal period may be uncertain. She has to acknowledge a sense of disappointment and even failure at having been unable to carry a baby to full term. In order to accomplish these psychological tasks, she must engage in some of the following problem-solving activities: She must prepare for possible loss of the baby with some anticipatory grief reaction such as sadness or depression. Denial of the real threat or too early an optimism and cheerfulness are considered risks from a mental health point of view. Since a sense of guilt and self-blame is frequently aroused, the mother must be able to deal actively with such feelings in order to reduce their intensity and possible later negative effects.

Phase 2. The mother is at home; the infant remains in premature nursery. The psychological tasks require the development of some hope that the infant will survive and will be home soon. It requires recognition that a premature infant needs special care, but that eventually the needs and characteristics of the infant will be that of a normal child. The problem-solving activities require that the mother take an active interest in the details of the progress of the baby while in the nursery and that she prepare for its needs.

Phase 3. The infant is now at home. The chief psychological task is the establishment of a tender and nurturing relationship between mother and infant, which has been ruptured by the premature birth and in some instances by long separation. The problem-solving tasks require the assumption of the nurturing role, attention and sensitivity to special needs, and (in some instances) coping realistically with congenital abnormalities frequently found in prematures.

On the basis of preliminary study, certain patterns have been identified which are considered maladaptive and which prognosticate a poor outcome to the crisis. For example, some mothers deny heavily both the threat to life and the implications of maternal failure. Some fail to respond with hope to indications that the infant will survive. Some have no interest in the details of the baby's development and may refuse to visit or be active in securing information about the baby's growth.

DESCRIPTION OF THE STUDY

The following observations are based on work with 11 families comprising a total of sixty interviews, all held in the home.[8] In addition, there were contacts with health and welfare agencies in behalf of some of the families.

The case-finding aspects of the project were handled as follows: A psychiatrist staff member developed liaison with the city hospital and was notified of all premature births.[9] During the period of case-find-

---

[6] This concept will seem particularly at variance with traditionalist psychiatric views.

[7] These concepts were developed by David Kaplan at the Family Guidance Center, Harvard School of Public Health, and are described in "Predicting Outcome from Situational Stress on the Basis of Individual Problem-solving Patterns." Ph.D. thesis, University of Minnesota, 1961.

[8] Five families of the 11 were visited by a graduate student from the Smith College School for Social Work, supervised by the author.

[9] Dr. Edward Mason, who also served as consultant to this study.

3

ing for this study, he interviewed mothers on the ward soon after delivery. These interviews were brief and were not traditional psychiatric interviews with intent of probing. Instead the aim was twofold. First, to make a rapid assessment of the mother's (and when available, the family's) reaction to the current stressful event; to note coping mechanisms with which the stress was being handled; and to make predictions at this early stage regarding the outcome, to be verified later. Second, to obtain sanction for a social worker to visit the family in the home in order to follow developments and offer any help that might be needed. It should be noted that because of hospital regulations the social worker, coming from an outside agency, was not permitted to visit and work with the mothers in the hospital. Therefore no work could be done with the mothers during the first important phase of the crisis.[10]

The families were then visited, whenever possible, during the first week following the mother's discharge from the hospital. The frequency, spacing, and duration of contacts were determined flexibly on the basis of assessment of the families' needs and were sustained wherever possible only until the crisis appeared resolved. The following three case examples are cited to illustrate the range of problems encountered and the kinds of intervention offered.

CASE ONE

The Brown family consisted of a young working-class Negro couple and their premature first-born baby. The mother was 17, the father 24. The baby was born during the seventh month, weighing 4 pounds and 4 ounces. The mother was seen twice by the project psychiatrist, on the second and fifth days after delivery. She was being treated for a kidney infection, which

[10] It may very well be that the inaccessibility of the mothers to the social worker during the stress impact period brought into focus some emotional tasks and needs during the second phase which might better have been resolved earlier.

explains her longer hospitalization. She was in a markedly sullen mood on both occasions, but did warm up to the doctor. She indicated to the worker later that this contact meant a great deal to her because she had an opportunity to talk to someone. She was quite worried about the baby's welfare, exasperated at not getting news, but unable to be insistent in making inquiries. She became more anxious on hearing of the death of a smaller premature infant. She tended to blame overwork, not taking vitamins, and the kidney infection as possible causes for the premature delivery. On the basis of her concern, her ability to express normal anxiety, and her wish to have the baby home soon, it was predicted that she would make a good relationship with the baby and would be a competent mother, although somewhat anxious.

There were six home visits, numerous phone calls, and contacts with health agencies regarding the Brown family. The first visit occurred one week after the mother's discharge from the hospital, at the paternal grandparents' home. The mother was able to express disappointment that the baby was not yet home. Despite a characteristic guardedness, abruptness, and sullen, hostile defense displayed at each contact, she soon warmed up and was eager to discuss the baby, and asked very specific questions. The father was acutely uncomfortable, taciturn, and soon fled from the interview. He was not seen again, and the next visits were focused on the mother's needs.

In the first interview the mother was still troubled with feelings of guilt and responsibility for the baby's early arrival, which had caught her unprepared, especially psychologically. She did not get a chance to wear her new maternity suit, which meant she really did not have a long enough period as young wife without motherhood. Nevertheless, she was eager to get the baby home, was defensive about not having visited, and took pride in the layette she was readying. She and her husband visited subsequently until the baby's discharge. She was appro-

4

priately anxious, in view of her inexperience, about the care of the baby. It was the worker's initial impression that she would have ample help from extended family and public health nurses. This was an erroneous impression. The female family members were not helpful and no public health nurse or well-baby clinic was available in this town. The worker's role therefore became primarily an educational one. The mother was extremely eager to learn and was found to be very responsive and educable. The emphasis was on helping her find ways of getting information she needed as well as on supplying basic knowledge of infant care and development.

The second visit, a long one, was scheduled the day after the baby came home at the age of 4 weeks. Gradually the mother's uncertainties unfolded. She was alone with the newborn, had never made a formula, was worried about room temperature and about his weight. She was upset by his diaper rash, blamed the hospital for negligence, and changed his diapers every fifteen minutes, washing them by hand. She gave the baby orange juice and vitamins, and had little idea of quantity; a month later it was learned that she was giving the baby concentrated undiluted orange juice, which explained his diarrhea. This happened despite carefully detailed discussions regarding routines. Her attitude toward the baby was one of great concern and wanting to do right. She did not appear overly warm or maternal, yet was attentive to the baby's communications and needs.

On subsequent visits more concerns were expressed, despite the fact that the baby was progressing well. The hospital discharged the mother with some printed instructions she had not read: they were in small print and hard to understand. The worker presented her with a copy of Spock's baby book. Some of the language was found to be geared to middle-class education and sophistication. Worker and mother studied the book together; the latter was charmed with the pictures, and learned to

use the index. She was eager to make use of health facilities but needed precise information as to how to initiate things. When told exactly, she always followed through. With the worker's active intervention and enlistment of the help of medical social workers at a private pediatric hospital, the baby was taken on for care. The mother followed through, although it required a long trip to a strange community. Despite careful preparation, as with the orange juice, communication failed. The mother went to the hospital without the baby to inquire about eligibility. This was misinterpreted by the medical personnel as an expression of her suspiciousness and resistance. The worker's active and rapid clarification once again smoothed the pathway for this family to develop good patterns of health care.

CASE TWO

The Kellys, an Irish Catholic working-class family, are an example of prediction of a healthy outcome, confirmed by three follow-up visits. The mother delivered a 4-pound premature boy and a stillborn male twin of 12 ounces. Her water bag had broken two months previously and she was carefully followed prenatally. A premature birth had been anticipated, but not a stillborn twin. When interviewed briefly by the project psychiatrist three days after delivery, she had already seen the baby three times through the glass of the nursery. She had three children under 6 at home. She was able to express concern about the needs of the newborn and was eager to get some idea of when he might come home. She was active in "pestering" doctors and nurses to seek out information about the baby, who was jaundiced and edematous. On the basis of the mother's ability to mourn for the dead twin, to express open concern for the surviving infant, to seek medical information aggressively, and to use warmth and support of the extended family and religious institutions, it was predicted that the outcome of the crisis would be excellent

5

and the mother-child relationship satisfactory. There was no need for preventive intervention, but follow-up was initiated for research purposes and to verify the prediction.

The first visit was made five weeks after delivery. An earlier visit failed to locate the family, who had no telephone. The parents were pleased to see the worker, despite the fact that the visit was unscheduled and the mother in bed with flu. Noteworthy were the parents' ease in communication with each other and the worker and their spontaneous ability to recount in detail, with appropriate affect, the painful events of pregnancy, precipitous birth, the death of the twin, and the prolonged hospitalization of the baby. Before her current illness the mother had visited the baby three times. The father visited daily. More remarkable was their active communication with the medical staff. It was against hospital policy to give telephone information even to parents. Nevertheless the pediatrician frequently telephoned the parents at a neighbor's. The baby was in the hospital longer than anticipated because of anemia, necessitating blood transfusions. During the second visit, five weeks later, the mother was seen alone. The baby was still not at home because of the blood level and need for surgery for umbilical hernia. The striking feature was the mother's active seeking and using medical knowledge as a way of mastering the crisis. She was appropriately concerned, but also optimistic. There was a definite reduction in her level of tension, despite the disappointment of the long hospitalization.

The third visit, one month later, found the family at home, elated and happy. The baby had been home a fortnight. Prior to his actual homecoming they had suffered a needless trauma due to communication failure; they were told to get the baby and went with great anticipation, only to learn it was an error. They came home, again empty-handed; were disappointed and depressed. This reactivated the original disappointment and loss, but gave them a second chance to work out the mourning process. Now they were relieved and less anxious, even coping comfortably with the baby's colic. It may be noted that from the beginning the infant had an identity and place in the family. He was "little Joey" and was talked about easily and freely. In this last contact with the worker the opportunity was created for the family to relive once again the whole experience from beginning to end. The fortuitous outcome in this case, despite long hospitalization and medical complications, was related to the family's close ties, shared goals, communication patterns, and capacity for conscious problem-solving. The mother had a high degree of interpersonal skills and was able to handle medical personnel in order to get needed information. She did this aggressively but with kidding and lightness of touch, managing her own anxiety and thus avoiding stimulating the feelings of guilt of professional personnel, which so often result in their withdrawal and withholding. Despite the mother's experience in raising babies, she welcomed the possibility of visits by the public health nurse and used the social worker constructively for abreaction and mastery.

CASE THREE

The Minellis, an Italian Catholic working-class family, illustrate the need for long-term intervention dictated by the fact that the current crisis was superimposed on chronic family problems and repeated crises which were the characteristic family life style. On the basis of two brief contacts in the hospital, the first with the husband present, the project psychiatrist in his prediction expressed uneasiness about the family's adjustment to the new baby. There were indications that the family needed to be visited, for there was danger of neglect for the baby. These ominous predictions were based on the following observations: The baby was born at seven months weighing 3 pounds. The parents insisted that

6

everything was fine and expected the baby to be home in a month. Two important facts stood out: This was the sixth premature child in the family, all of whom had survived. However, this infant had the smallest birth weight.

It might be expected that with this family history confidence and hope might be high.[11] On the other hand, the expectation of the baby's homecoming in a month showed evidence of unrealistic thinking and denial in view of the extensive prior experience with prematurity. There were other indications of denial. The husband, particularly, did not permit his wife or himself to express any feelings of anxiety. He insisted that once the baby began to eat everything would be all right. When the wife was seen alone without the repressive presence of her husband, she was indeed visibly more anxious but still clung to her denial defenses. For example, at the time of delivery she had been ill with a strep throat, but denied its significance. There was indication that the mother had some real conflict about this baby. Prediction therefore was of a dubious outcome and guarded prognosis.

All the early cues of a very troubled family situation and problematic mother-child relationship were unfortunately confirmed. The family was visited five days after delivery, when the mother had been at home two days. During this visit the family presented a solid, united, euphoric front. The father handled his anxiety regarding the newborn by boasting of the good health and strong development of the other children. Later it was found that all the children had numerous health problems, some severe, all of which were being neglected. The mother was taking expensive medicine (antibiotics)

—her "Christmas present"—not knowing what it was for. Her husband's fantasy was that it would "heal up her insides." The parents hardly discussed the baby. The nurse in the premature nursery reported that the mother had shown no interest in the baby and had not come down to visit while she was in the hospital.

This family was visited twenty times, with numerous phone contacts and collaborative contacts with health agencies. Every area of their social functioning was problematic and chaotic. They were in severe and chronic financial difficulties despite the husband's fairly steady and well-paid employment. The children were malnourished and chronically hungry. They were periodically threatened with loss of utilities and eviction by the housing project. There were periodic altercations with neighbors and recriminations in court. Two of the school-aged children were slow learners and were threatened with being left back in school. All children had uncared-for health problems; they were in need of eye surgery, tonsillectomies, orthopedic attention, and polio shots.

There were severe problems also in the mother's inability to manage and control the children. The older ones were defiant and attacking. The mother handled discipline by explosive outbursts, ineffectual threats, bribery, and virtual encouragement of the children to lie and steal. There were severe marital problems. The mother was terrified of another pregnancy but could not handle the sexual relationship because of internal conflicts and external religious prohibitions regarding birth control. The husband was depressed and disgruntled with his job and plagued by physical symptoms for which he refused medical attention. The extended family was in proximity but could offer no help.

The baby was very slow in his development both at the hospital and at home, despite the absence of any abnormalities. For example, at 6 weeks he weighed only 3 pounds and 11 ounces. At 8 weeks he came

---

[11] A finding of the research project revealed that prior experience with prematurity was not a significant factor in the outcome of the crisis. Birth weight as a factor showed surprisingly that the outcome of the family crisis was better with smaller premature infants than larger ones. *See* Kaplan, *op. cit.*, p. 115.

7

home weighing 5 pounds and 2 ounces. The relief about this was noted by the mother only in terms of the children having quieted down. The mother had visited the baby in hospital only once, and only at the worker's urging. She did not visit at the time of her postnatal check-up. The baby's subsequent slow development was of concern. He was extremely lethargic, apathetic, and unresponsive, making few demands of any kind. He was given very cursory and minimal handling. His bottle rolled around in the crib and whoever passed by might pop it in his mouth. In contrast to many mothers of premature babies who are overly concerned with diet and push feeding, this mother seemed unconcerned and unable to request help with change of formula even after months had elapsed, although her other children's diet at a comparable age had been enriched. The baby received very little handling and stimulation and was picked up and held, briefly at best, only with the worker's encouragement. He did not have a real place in the family, and began to be identified by name only at the age of 6 months. The mother found very little pleasure in him. She saw him in a positive way only insofar as he provided something for her—that is, he helped her "keep her mind off her worries." There was evidence that her greater attentiveness at night enabled her to use the baby as a way of avoiding sexual contact with her husband. She admitted that she had tried to abort him.

The contacts with this family had a multiple purpose. The primary task, in keeping with the research, was to focus on getting a relationship going between mother and infant—a relationship in this instance ruptured by the baby's prolonged separation while in hospital and further weakened by the fact of his being unwanted. Active intervention via encouragement and demonstration consisted of stimulating visiting, physical contact, and more adequate nurturing. The mother made fleeting efforts, but her responses were not sustained. Active intervention was also offered regarding health needs for the baby and other children, by opening contacts with public health nurses who had become hostile to this family. Rules were modified, fees were waived, and punitive or negative attitudes on the part of other caretaking personnel were modified by consultation and collaboration methods.

The secondary task (but of prime importance in this chronically disordered family) was to break through denial and inactivity and to involve them in beginning problem-solving and coping with urgent demands. Active intervention in this respect consisted of securing free school lunches, concrete help with budgeting, meal-planning, and management of debts; some demonstration of child management, since efforts at modifying attitudes and handling failed; pushing the mother out of her fruitless obsessional worrying by activating some beginning of coping with small pieces of problems and tasks; getting her out of the house, where she was characteristically immobilized over coffee and cigarettes and aimless fretting. It was recognized that this family would need long-term intervention for any sustained results. As is true of many chronically needy and dependent families, this one made no demands and did not make use of resources even when the family was eligible and the resources available to them. Most needs were handled by means of magical thinking and wish fulfillment, or frantic worrying leading to rumination and inactivity rather than direct action. The mother enjoyed the "friendly visiting," made no demands, held herself aloof and detached except for rare occasions when some genuine affect broke through and she turned to the worker to unburden.

The husband was seen less frequently. He managed to remove himself physically or refused to participate, encouraged by his wife, who tried to shield him from worries. Among the children, all but the oldest formed strong attachments to the worker, displayed their great hunger for affection and contact, and at times saw the worker

8

as the embodiment of standards and benign controls for which they still yearned despite the prevailing influences of corruption and chaos that ruled their lives.

SUMMARY AND CONCLUSION

These three cases illustrate a range of responses to the crisis of prematurity. In the first case the family's coping mechanisms were not adequate to the task essentially because of lack of knowledge. Intervention therefore was largely educational in purpose. The second case illustrates adequate coping with the crisis. The third case illustrates great inadequacy during the crisis— a cumulative product of chronic inadequacy which even extended preventive intervention failed to modify.

Preventive intervention with the families studied consisted of a range of activities. They can be classified into three broad categories.

1. Keeping an explicit focus on the crisis. Four specific goals may be subsumed in this category.

a. Help with cognitive mastery: not all families consciously perceive a hazardous event and their reactions to it as a time of family crisis. A major task of preventive intervention is to help the family gain a conscious grasp of the crisis, in order to enhance purposeful problem-solving, leading toward mastery. It has been noted by various investigators that clarification of the precipitating stress, or connection of subjective distress with stressful event, is in itself of therapeutic significance.[12]

b. Help with doubts of feminine adequacy, guilt, and self-blame stimulated by the failure to carry the pregnancy to term.

c. Help with grief work and mourning in relation to feelings of loss and emptiness stimulated by separation from the infant.

d. Help with anticipatory worry work and anticipatory guidance. These activities are carried on in the context of supportive and clarifying techniques with which social workers are familiar. Sometimes it is sufficient to work out the crisis on the level of the "here and now." At other times it may be necessary to make more explicit the symbolic link of the present crisis to earlier unresolved conflicts. These links may be difficult to establish within the context of a brief relationship which is not geared to conflict resolution, or clarification leading toward insight. Nevertheless, because of the pressure of the crisis, such conflicts or derivatives may surge nearer to consciousness and may be accessible to direct interpretation.

2. Offering basic information and education regarding child development and child care through a variety of devices, including use of relationship for demonstration and identification.

3. Creating a bridge to community resources, opening pathways of referral, and intervening in communication failures and in problems of stereotyping and misinterpretation of motivation and need.

[12] B. L. Kalis, M. R. Harris, A. R. Prestwood, and E. H. Freeman, "Precipitating Stress as a Focus in Psychotherapy," *Archives of General Psychiatry*, Vol. 5, No. 3 (September 1961), pp. 219–226.

This article describes three predictable and sequential phases that represent a normal cycle of emotional responses by victims of sexual assault: (1) acute reaction, (2) outward adjustment, and (3) integration and resolution of the experience. A series of interventions was developed to help patients work through each phase as smoothly as possible.

Crisis intervention with victims of rape

by Sandra Sutherland Fox and Donald J. Scherl, MD

Sandra Sutherland Fox, MSSA, is Codirector, Metropolitan Mental Health Skills Center, Washington, D.C., and Donald J. Scherl, MD, is Assistant Professor of Psychiatry, Harvard Medical School, and Director of Community Mental Health Services, Massachusetts Mental Health Center, Boston, Massachusetts.

Mental health workers often feel unprepared or unable to help groups of individuals whose acute or chronic emotional problems are outside the boundaries of their professional skills. Rape victims represent one such group. However, professionals learn a series of generic skills and, as their knowledge and experience broaden, they should be able to refine these skills and relate them to an array of specific problems. This article describes specific skills that may be used by mental health workers to help victims of rape.

During 1966 and 1967, thirteen rape victims were seen in a setting similar to that in which a crisis intervention team might be located—a community mental health facility, for example. All the victims were young, unmarried adult females whose past histories were consistent with psychological health and achievement. Although length of contact with these patients varied, most were seen within forty-eight hours of the assault. Thus it was possible to follow the majority of them during their acute reactions to the experience. As a result, the authors were able to identify a predictable pattern of responses common to these patients: (1) acute reaction, occurring immediately after the rape and usually lasting for several days, (2) outward adjustment, and (3) integration and resolution of the experience.[1] A series of specific mental health interventions was then designed to help the patients work through each phase as smoothly and completely as possible.

PHASE 1: ACUTE REACTION

Immediately following sexual assault, the victim's feelings include shock, disbelief, or dismay, followed by anxiety and fear. If she feels she did not invite the rape, i.e., she was not seductive or willingly compliant, she usually reports it to the police immediately or seeks medical attention. If neither of these steps is taken promptly, the

[1] Sandra Sutherland and Donald J. Scherl, MD, "Patterns of Response Among Victims of Rape," *American Journal of Orthopsychiatry*, Vol. 40, No. 3 (April 1970), pp. 503–511.

Reprinted from SOCIAL WORK, 17 (January 1972), pp. 37–42. Copyright © by the National Association of Social Workers, Inc., 1972.

CAO–010–C

worker should be alert to the possible diagnostic significance of her delay.

It is extremely important during Phase 1 for the worker to encourage the patient to talk about the assault. Often her relatives and friends try to dissuade her from thinking or talking about it in the mistaken belief that she will become more emotionally distressed. However, if others refuse to listen, the patient may conclude that they are embarrassed and ashamed and want to punish her for what has happened.

The worker must help the victim deal with the following issues during the acute phase: (1) medical attention, (2) legal matters and police contacts, (3) notification of family or friends, (4) current practical concerns, (5) clarification of factual information, (6) emotional responses, and (7) psychiatric consultation.

Medical attention. If the patient has not received medical attention when first seen by the mental health worker, arrangements for a physical examination should be made immediately to provide for the victim's health and any future medicolegal requirements. The examination should include tests for venereal disease and pregnancy. Since most pregnancy tests are negative until several weeks after conception, they are often postponed. However, they are valuable for legal purposes because they indicate whether the woman was already pregnant when the rape occurred.

The worker should know in advance which hospitals and clinics will accept rape victims and under what circumstances. Some will not treat such patients unless a police report has been filed; others are reluctant to become involved because of the time required for court appearances if the victim presses charges against her assailant.

Legal services and police contacts. Although the patient may not currently plan to press charges or take any legal action, the worker should encourage her to discuss her situation with an attorney immediately. This step is important because her feelings and plans will fluctuate in the future. Unless the worker has had special legal training, he should not give the patient specific legal advice. He should, however, help her to locate competent legal services.

If the assault has not been reported to the police, the victim must decide whether she will do so and what role she wants the worker to take in that process. She should be aware that if she reports the rape, she can expect to have extensive contact with the police. For example, she will be asked to answer questions about the assault, locate where it occurred, and identify the assailant in a lineup. If she is anxious about reporting the assault to the police, it is appropriate for the worker to accompany her.

If the woman decides not to report the rape, she should be aware of the possible consequences. In evaluating his own legal and moral obligations, the worker must remember that he has no proof, other than the alleged victim's statement, that a crime in fact occurred.

Notification of family and/or friends. The authors found that a rape victim's anxiety usually diminishes significantly after she has talked with a relative or friend about the assault. Thus the worker should help her decide who will be told (e.g., parents, fiancé, friend, clergyman) and how this will be accomplished. After deciding whom she will notify, the woman has several alternatives: she can handle the notification herself, call or talk with the person in the worker's presence, or ask the worker to talk to the person while she is present. If none of these choices are possible, the worker can notify the relative or friend after discussing with the victim what she wants said.

As a general rule, the victim should do as much as possible herself. However, if she is unable to take any necessary step, she should be present when that step is handled for her. This will reduce her opportunities to misunderstand, distort, and fantasize about what the worker has said or done.

Current practical concerns. As part of meeting the victim's emotional needs, the worker should help her deal with current practical problems. For example, she

2

should be prepared for possible publicity and the steps she can take to maintain her privacy. If the assault has already been publicized, she should know how to respond to possible questions. Other practical problems involve repair of windows, doors, and locks; money for the patient's immediate needs (if she has been robbed); and what she can do if she becomes frightened. By dealing with these details, the victim begins to "detoxify" the experience and temporarily sets it behind her. When this occurs, she enters Phase 2.

Clarification of basic information. It is important for the patient to understand the implications of what has happened to her. For example, one young woman who was unusually anxious during her initial interview with the social worker finally sobbed that she did not want to be pregnant. When the worker said it was impossible to tell at that point whether she was pregnant, the patient was astonished because she had thought all intercourse resulted in pregnancy. Although such serious misunderstandings are rare, the worker should be sure the victim's fund of information is adequate and accurate.

Emotional responses. To respond appropriately to the issues that are psychologically relevant to the patient during Phase 1, the mental health worker must be willing to help her cope with both her feelings and reality. Thus an attitude of warmth, calmness, empathy, and firm consistency is likely to be most useful, i.e., the worker must be personally involved yet professionally objective. Because he must deal with the patient's emotional crisis as it manifests itself in both her behavior and affect, he would be as wrong to listen passively to her as he would be to guide her actively.

In the early part of the relationship, the worker may have to see the patient daily. Hours of his time may be spent on activities such as arranging for medical care, making a referral for legal services, helping the patient with police requirements, or just listening to her—all of which are valid uses of his time and energy. The worker will also want to formulate some tentative diagnostic impressions about why this person was assaulted at this specific time and place and assess the victim's strengths and limitations. These insights will help him understand the diagnostic meaning of the rape to the patient, which in turn will aid him in formulating a treatment plan.

Anticipatory guidance is an additional skill that is often useful in helping a rape victim not only to understand what she is currently experiencing, but to respond appropriately to the impact of later phases. Because a healthy single woman's emotional responses to rape are predictable, the worker should discuss them with her. The victim should be assured that her feelings are similar to those experienced by other women in her situation and that after several days or weeks she will be able to return to her usual activities feeling less troubled (Phase 2). She should also realize that most women go through a third phase in which they feel depressed and mentally relive the experience. The worker should also give her the names of available mental health resources in case she needs further professional help during Phase 3.

Psychiatric consultation. Although a psychiatrist should be consulted about each case, he will not need to be involved directly with the patient in most instances. However, when diagnostic, medicolegal, or clinical issues merit psychiatric evaluation or intervention or the patient requests a psychiatric interview, he should become actively involved. For example, a psychiatrist would be helpful in evaluating the patient's current mental status or underlying pathology or in determining whether specific responses are normal or psychopathological.

PHASE 2: OUTWARD ADJUSTMENT

As the victim deals with practical problems, various psychological mechanisms such as denial of affect, suppression, and rationalization are called into play. She resumes her normal activities and appears to be adjusting to the assault. Her interest in seeking help and talking about her experience wanes rapidly. This response is healthy and should be encouraged, despite the fact that it represents an interim period of pseudoadjustment.

The worker's appropriate role in Phase 2 is one of support rather than challenge. Although he may be tempted to challenge the patient's defenses, such interference is unproductive and unsound. Final resolution and integration come later, after the patient has worked through the experience during Phase 3; thus her emotional reactions should be allowed to run their course.

Unless the woman requests specific help, there is relatively little for the worker to do during Phase 2. He should encourage the patient to keep her follow-up medical appointments. However, because she denies the emotional impact of the assault and feels it is best forgotten, she will often fail to keep these appointments.

During Phase 2, the worker may have additional opportunities to work with the patient's relatives or friends, who may want to talk with someone after helping the patient through the acute crisis. Often they feel that the woman has been "ruined" and may convey this to her so strongly that it becomes part of her self-image. They may be extremely angry with the patient, feeling that she was seductive, careless, or did not heed their warnings. In such situations, the worker can help these relatives or friends realistically evaluate the rape and their own reactions to it.

As in Phase 1, anticipatory guidance is important because most patients do not expect to experience further emotional reactions. The worker should describe the feelings that rape victims normally experience during Phase 3 and assure the patient that mental health resources will be available if she needs them.

Sometimes a rape victim will seek help for the first time during Phase 2, usually because a friend or relative urged her to do so. However, the patient generally is reluctant to involve herself in an intensive helping relationship at this time and should not be criticized for her feelings. The worker can help her gain perspective about

her current reaction by describing Phases 1 and 3 and can offer psychiatric services if she requests such help. It is also helpful if the worker talks with the relative or friend who urged the victim to seek help. The aim of such an interview is to counsel the person about the victim's current status and predictable future reactions and to give him an opportunity to discuss his own feelings.

PHASE 3: INTEGRATION

When Phase 3 begins the patient usually feels depressed and wants to talk. She should again be reassured that such feelings are predictable and usually do not indicate serious emotional problems. Arrangements for counseling can appropriately be made at this time.

Frequently, a specific incident precipitates Phase 3, for example, the patient finds she is pregnant, receives a court summons, or sees a man who resembles her assailant. In such cases, the worker should direct his initial efforts toward helping the patient deal with the precipitating factor and discuss her feelings with her after the practical problem has been resolved. When there is no identifiable precipitant to Phase 3, the victim seeks help because she finds she is constantly thinking about the assault and wonders why.

In the third phase, two central issues must be worked through with the victim: her feelings about herself and her feelings about the assailant. Often she feels guilty, unclean, or damaged, and it is useless for the worker to reassure her until she has talked about these feelings. Although the worker may believe there was nothing the woman could have done to prevent the attack, he must be cautious about saying so. It is preferable for the victim to reach this conclusion (if it is an accurate one) on her own, guided by appropriate questions from the worker. Some patients need to go through a period of guilt and self-punishment as a first step toward integrating the experience. If the worker challenges their guilt prematurely, such patients often feel

4

he does not understand and therefore cannot help them. If a patient does bear partial responsibility for the assault, she must be helped to understand her behavior before she can fully integrate the experience.

The victim's feelings of being dirty or despoiled may be more difficult to deal with. If she continues to be troubled by such feelings, a psychiatric consultation should be arranged to evaluate their origin and prognostic significance, and, if necessary, psychiatric treatment should be initiated.

The second major issue to be resolved during Phase 3 concerns the victim's feelings about her assailant. Her initial feelings of anger—denied, suppressed, or rationalized during Phase 2—now reappear for resolution. Frequently, her anger toward the assailant is distorted into anger toward herself, which exacerbates the characteristic depression of this phase. Thus it is important for the worker to "permit" the patient to express this anger.

The victim's depression, fear, and anxiety can be considered within normal limits if her depression is reactive, time limited, and nonpsychotic. Further careful evaluation is needed if her normal sleeping or eating patterns are disrupted, she suffers from generalized fears, or indulges in compulsive rituals.

The type of mental health services the patient needs during Phase 3 depends on her personality structure and how easily and completely she has experienced Phases 1 and 2. Although it may be necessary for the worker to see the patient frequently at the beginning of this phase to help her deal with specific problems or crises, appointments can soon be scheduled on a regular basis. Such an approach will help the victim perceive her own strengths and ability to cope with her problems. It will also help to dilute her feelings of crisis, which should be discouraged in this phase. If such feelings persist, a psychiatric consultation is advisable.

Usually Phase 3 is relatively brief. After several weeks most women have integrated the experience and it takes its appropriate place in the past. If the patient does not accomplish this within a reasonable period, her response is probably not within normal limits; i.e., the rape has created or rearoused feelings that the ego cannot handle without the development of symptoms at the psychotic, neurotic, or behavioral level. In such cases, the worker must evaluate the degree of stress involved in the experience and its aftermath and the ego's capacity to cope with stress of that magnitude.

Occasionally a rape victim seeks professional help for the first time during Phase 3. In such cases it is important for the worker to understand why the victim asked for help and what the specific reasons are for her emotional discomfort. In addition to the issues usually dealt with in Phase 3, it is helpful if the worker discusses with the patient her reactions to date and how she has dealt with them. If she can relive the shock, anxiety, and dismay of Phase 1 and be reassured that these reactions are normal and predictable, it will be easier for her to resolve the issues that normally arise during Phase 3 and integrate the total experience. All women seen during Phase 3 should be reassured about the continued availability of mental health resources.

CONCLUSION

As a result of their work with a number of young, unmarried adult victims of rape, the authors were able to delineate three predictable and sequential phases that apparently represent a normal cycle of emotional responses to sexual assault. Using this knowledge, the authors then developed a series of interventions to help these patients work through these phases successfully. The response patterns described provide only a general context in which to help such patients; the detailed contents for individual patients were as varied as their personalities, backgrounds, and experiences. Thus no one victim required each intervention described.

Although rape victims represent a specific group, the generic skills to help them are included in the repertoires of most me

5

health workers and are general enough to use with diverse groups of patients. In any treatment situation a meaningful conceptual framework must be developed to understand the patient's emotional reactions so that the necessary countermeasures can be applied.

One important question that remains unanswered is whether the information gathered by the authors has implications for the prevention of rape. For example, if a woman enters a socioeconomic or cultural area different from her own, she should anticipate how her presence will be interpreted by those who live there. By understanding her own behavior and how it is perceived by others, and by knowing how to avoid communicating inappropriate cues, it is possible that rape could sometimes be avoided. Although the sample size was not large enough to justify any broad generalizations, the information described in this article may have useful applications in preventing such crimes.

BY JEANETTE R. OPPENHEIMER

Use of Crisis Intervention in Casework with the Cancer Patient and His Family

■ Cancer, an emotionally charged illness, can be expected to precipitate a state of crisis for most patients and their families. An understanding of crisis theory and the phenomena that occur during a state of crisis are basic to the social worker's approach to the problems the cancer patient presents. The techniques for intervention and change are focused on (1) helping the patient or family develop conscious awareness of their problem, (2) assessing their total situation, and (3) enabling them to make a new use of their existing ego-adaptive techniques or to develop new and more effective mechanisms. ■

PROFOUND CHANGES IN the nature and treatment of illness have been produced by the advances in medical science that have taken place in the last twenty-five years. Recent discoveries, new methods of diagnosis, and refinements in therapeutic techniques have resulted in total cures for some diseases, the almost complete eradication of others, and in some, such as tuberculosis, a change in the concept of therapy and a reduction in the incidence of the disease itself. Even the complex of diseases called "cancer" has been influenced.

Social work service for the cancer patient and his family reflects these medical advances. Cancer is an emotionally charged illness that can affect every area of an individual's life experience. Because of the implications this diagnosis has for the patient and his family, it is often viewed as a crisis of high magnitude and stress. An understanding of crisis theory and the phenomena that occur during a state of crisis is basic to the social worker's approach to the problems the cancer patient presents.

CRISIS THEORY

Harriett Bartlett has stated: "The stressfulness of illness and medical care is beyond the adjustive capacity of many individuals."[1] The diagnosis of cancer with all of its implications can be counted on to precipitate a state of crisis of varying intensity and duration for nearly every patient and his family. The social worker must recognize the nature of the threat this diagnosis constitutes and what enters into an effort to establish equilibrium for the patient and his family. It is true that cancer, its associated therapeutic processes, and the characteristic manifestations of the spread of the disease may continue to produce obstacles to resolution of the crisis for some patients and their families, whose situation becomes a chronically demoralizing experience. By

JEANETTE R. OPPENHEIMER, MS, is Director, Department of Social Work, Roswell Park Memorial Institute, Buffalo, New York. An earlier version of this paper was presented at a meeting of the Cuyahoga Unit, American Cancer Society, in Cleveland, Ohio, February 1963.

[1] Harriett M. Bartlett, "The Widening Scope of Hospital Social Work," Social Casework, Vol. 44, No. 1 (January 1963), p. 6.

contrast, many individuals and their families, even though aware of impending death and permanent separation from a loved one, are able to develop solutions beyond their customary range of problem-solving mechanisms. Thus, some patients achieve a level of adaptation that enables them to cope with the many threats to their equilibrium throughout the course of their illness, and the surviving family is able to make an adequate adjustment.

Insights gained from the concepts of ego psychology, psychoanalytic precepts, and social role theory are implicit in the use of crisis intervention techniques that form the basis for social casework treatment of cancer patients and their families. In some situations, because of the nature of the person-problem-situation configuration, it may be more appropriate to select another treatment method based on recognition of the need for a sustained relationship over a long period of time. The focus here may be on problems in interpersonal relationships or on serious pre-existing neurotic patterns that inhibit the patient's capacity to use appropriate medical care for the treatment of his disease. For those individuals whose disease runs a lengthy course (a phenomenon occurring more frequently with the use of new drugs and more radical surgical procedures) there may be periods of remission and relapse with each episode of recurrence likely to produce new and more frightening or disabling symptoms. These episodes may necessitate the use of social work help again as the patient needs further assistance in coping with a new dimension of the original crisis.

The techniques for intervention and change in this crisis situation, as in other crises, are focused on (1) helping the patient or family develop conscious awareness of their problem, (2) assessing quickly and accurately the total situation for patient and family, and (3) enabling the patient and family to make a new use of their existing ego-adaptive techniques or to develop new and more effective mechanisms.

AWARENESS OF THE PROBLEM

The basic task for the patient is development of a conscious awareness of his problem, especially in the absence of his formal request for assistance. In a medical setting a social worker frequently finds himself in the predicament of beginning with a patient who has not voluntarily sought help, either because he is not consciously aware that he has a problem or, if he is aware of it, does not know where to take it. Lack of awareness may stem from deep but disguised anxiety manifested by assumption of a superficial guise of indifference. In the presence of a diagnosis such as cancer, which is so frequently equated with disaster, the patient's failure to initiate a request for help substantiates this view.

If the patient has been referred to the social worker by another individual (usually a doctor or a nurse), other elements enter the situation immediately, for example, who made the referral, why it was made, and how the referring individual defined for the patient why the referral was being made. Using the basic principle of casework practice, that of starting where the patient is, the content and quality of the referral presentation offer the first clue to his ego-functioning, as does the speed with which he sought medical care following the occurrence of significant physical symptomatology. The patient's reactions to the referral, whether denial, defensiveness, or resistance, are of diagnostic significance in understanding his personality and assessing the problem to be worked on. Often the referring individual does not give the patient adequate explanation to prepare him for the social worker, a situation that may well add to his confusion and anxiety. On the other hand, careful explanation by the referring individual may go unheeded if the degree of stress the patient is experiencing is too pervasive. Since the patient's capacity to participate and the extent of his involvement in meeting the crisis hinge on his awareness of his problem, the worker must determine the pa-

2

tient's ability to accept reality. Insight into his perceptive capacity may be gained if the worker can learn what part the patient had in identifying his problem to the referring individual. The apparent impact on him of his need for referral for social work help may offer further insights.

Many physicians are reluctant to inform the patient directly that he has cancer although they may indicate the serious nature of his illness to him in a vague way. According to Dr. James R. Nicholas, many physicians do, however, reveal the nature of the patient's illness to him by nonverbal means.[2] Usually patients sense the diagnosis or its implications. In spite of what appears to be denial or disinterest, most patients have some awareness of their medical problem, which they may need to reveal by nonverbal means. The worker must therefore be sensitive to signs or innuendoes that reveal this knowledge and indicate the patient's awareness of at least part of his problem. In the process of arriving at a diagnostic appraisal of the patient the worker must be alert to the defenses the patient may be developing, which represent various patterns of the ego's adaptation to stress, such as the use of denial. The worker should be aware of the value denial can have for the patient in coping with the situation and be able to leave him with this unless it is of such a crippling nature that it interferes with his use of medical care or ability to make any adjustment to his illness.

In some medical settings patients are not referred individually but are routinely interviewed by social workers when they are initially diagnosed as having cancer or are seen in a tumor clinic. The skill and sensitivity of the caseworker in initiating the first interview with the patient can often enable the patient to define his problem. If he has been newly diagnosed, the stress of the situation and his obvious anxiety give more readily discernible clues about the meaning his illness has for him before his defensive barrier has been erected and the process of adaptation begun. It is here that the worker may intervene effectively to prevent the development of maladaptive behavior that may intensify the crisis and make it less amenable to resolution.

The author's experience has been that when children have been diagnosed as having cancer prior to entering the hospital, their parents' defenses are up and the coping mechanism is already in operation, so that unless their problem-solving resources are inadequate or the new treatment procedure introduces an urgent new problem to be faced there may be a reluctance to begin social work treatment in a meaningful way. If, however, the diagnosis is initially established or incontrovertibly confirmed by the hospital's medical staff, so that the parents' last vestige of hope that their child does not have a malignant disease has been destroyed, they are more ready to acknowledge the existence of the problem and to begin to accept help in coping with their situation.

When the child has received treatment elsewhere (most frequently in a general hospital where he is apt to have been the only young patient with a fatal illness) before being referred to a specialized center, maladaptive behavior is often observed in both child and parents. This appears to be the result of a combination of the emotional attitudes of the professional staff caring for the child and failure of the parents to use or seek help. By the time the child is accepted for care, the maladaptive patterns may be well established and inaccessible to change in spite of intensive effort by all members of the medical team responsible for both medical and social treatment.

Most parents are haunted by awareness that immediate hospitalization may be necessary with the resultant need to cope with the child's anxiety about this possibility or his fear of medical procedures.

---

[2] James R. Nicholas, MD, "How a Patient with Cancer Learns the Diagnosis," *G.P.*, Vol. 32, No. 2 (August 1965), pp. 85–88.

3

Some parents are so lacking in ego strength that their only solution is in flight, which takes the form of failure to bring the child back for clinic care or to consult a physician in their own community.

ASSESSING THE SITUATION

As the social worker considers the cancer patient in order to arrive at a comprehensive understanding of him and of the crisis situation that exists for him and his family, to define with him the problem to be worked on, and to determine the processes that seem to offer the most promise for resolution of the problem, certain facts must be ascertained. What kinds of stresses are operating for the patient, both internally and externally? What adaptive mechanisms are already operating? How is the patient behaving in this crisis and how has he coped with other crises in the past? What is the patient's capacity for developing a meaningful relationship with the caseworker? What resources within the patient's environment may be counted on for help with solving the problem? The same diagnostic approach must apply to the patient's family or significant individuals in his immediate environment, since their response to the crisis must be considered in the treatment plan if there is to be any possibility for change.

The social worker must attempt to obtain an accurate picture of the patient's actual life situation, including an estimate of his physical condition, the extent of the disability, and immediate and long-range prognosis. Florence Hollis suggests that too often reliance is placed on the patient's spontaneous verbalization and that the worker is satisfied with generalizations instead of inquiring about the specifics on which the generalizations are based.[3] The worker should not be hesitant about asking for specific narrative detail.

Parad and Caplan's framework for study of the family in crisis is of particular value in work with the cancer patient and his family since it places emphasis on obtaining data that provide insight into (1) the family life-style as revealed in their value system, communication network, and role system, (2) intermediate problem-solving mechanisms that demonstrate the way in which they cope with situational stress, and (3) their need-response pattern, or the ways in which they perceive, respect, and satisfy the needs of individual family members.[4]

FAMILY ROLE RELATIONSHIPS

No comprehensive perception of the crisis situation for this group is possible unless knowledge has been gained of the role relationships that have existed for and between the patient and other meaningful individuals. Reuben Hill in his classification of stressor events that occur in family crises arising from "dismemberment" cites the marked change in the family configuration (though not a change in the plurality pattern) that is associated with prolonged hospitalization and with roles involuntarily vacated through illness.[5] Families of cancer patients are especially vulnerable to this because of the threat of the death of the patient or his need for special consideration and the fact that often his role in the family must be assumed by another. Furthermore, Hill points out that this type of crisis in the family sooner or later involves demoralization since the family's role patterns are sharply disturbed.[6] Since the

[3] Florence Hollis, "Personality Diagnosis in Casework," in Howard J. Parad, ed., *Ego Psychology and Dynamic Casework* (New York: Family Service Association of America, 1958), p. 88.

[4] Howard J. Parad and Gerald Caplan, "A Framework for Studying Families in Crisis," *Social Work*, Vol. 5, No. 3 (July 1960), pp. 6–8.

[5] While the sick individual is still viewed as a family member in terms of its size and constellation, his prolonged absence because of hospitalization or incapacity often leads to involuntary abdication of role. If this role remains unfilled or is assumed by another family member, a change in the family configuration results. Reuben Hill, "Generic Features of Families Under Stress," *Social Casework*, Vol. 39, Nos. 2–3 (February–March 1958), pp. 139–150.

[6] *Ibid.*, p. 146.

4

degree to which the patient and his family adjust depends to such a large extent on the adequacy of the role performance of each family member, they need to learn how to shift the role expectations they conceive for themselves and each other and how to work out different patterns in affectional and emotion-satisfying performances.

Needs of siblings. When the patient is a child, the needs of his siblings may not be met because the parents concentrate on trying to meet the emotional needs of the patient. Even though they may have made seemingly adequate provision for the care of their other children, siblings of patients frequently experience stress over and above their anxiety or guilt feelings about the patient, because they are deprived of the nurturing they would otherwise receive from their parents. This compounds the strain on the parents, who frequently are conflicted in their attempts to cope with the special needs of the fatally ill child and the needs of their well children. Some parents cannot bring themselves to discuss this; others handle their concern by denying the possibility that any dislocation can occur in the family situation. Some, who appear to be coping more adequately, try to divide their time between the patient and his siblings in an effort to meet the needs of the entire family as realistically as possible. Whatever the decision the parents make, the social worker endeavors to support them in their choice and to encourage them to be resourceful in finding ways to meet the needs of the entire family.

Assumption of patient role. It is important to understand what the role relationships were prior to the patient's illness, especially in respect to how the patient takes on and carries the role of a patient or relinquishes it. The addition of the patient role provides a coloration to the family's role performance that must be gauged if the worker is to comprehend the full meaning of the situation for them. The addition of this emotionally charged and threatening illness to the normal role system and the additional role the patient takes on may well lead to disequilibrium and thence to the demoralization described by Hill. One must, however, also recognize that some individuals and/or families gain new satisfactions in the patient role since it serves to meet long-existing but previously unfulfilled needs. For many patients the reverse is true. In his role as a patient the individual may well expect to be considered helpless and deserving of sympathy and tender care, and that the others in the family will take on protective nursing functions and attitudes. These actions and attitudes, however, do not always come spontaneously from family members, who are charged with his care while simultaneously being affected by his abdication of his customary role. They may resent the onerous duties placed on them and the patient's release from his own duties. By contrast, the too-ready response by the family to the patient in his new role may create further problems for him as he experiences the loss of a role that had deep meaning; he may feel no longer needed or valued.

Now that many patients are treated on an outpatient basis by chemotherapy or radiation therapy, the social worker may find that this conflicts with the patient and his family's concept of his role as a patient and as an extremely ill person. Consequently the crisis may center about their concept of how his role should be carried and the ensuing conflict that stems from the physician's differing concept and recommendations for treatment. The entire focus of the attempt to help resolve the problem may be on the process of enabling the patient and his family to develop a new perception of the problem with which they must cope—that of relinquishing the more passive inpatient role for that of an outpatient expected to meet many of his own needs and able to provide self-care.

Stresses on the patient. The surgical procedures that are often necessary in the treatment of cancer make severe demands

Social Work

5

on the individual's perception of his body-image and require him to adjust to radical changes in his body functions, thus creating additional areas of stress for him. Fastidious individuals are often initially repelled by colostomies and the new process of defecation they must learn. Women who have had mastectomies may feel that they have less value as females and may become anxious about their relationship with their husbands or, if single and of marriageable age, fearful of losing their ability to be attractive to men. Finally, surgical procedures involving the reproductive organs of either male or female patients may serve to arouse guilt feelings in the patient concerning the origin of the disease or in the spouse because of the sexual relationship with the patient.

In determining both the stresses present for the cancer patient and the resources available to him, the social worker must be mindful of additional external stresses that are a reflection of the attitudes of significant persons toward the diagnosis. The feelings of some family members about cancer as well as those of others in the patient's environment, including employers, teachers, and friends, may be a source of additional stress for him. For example, on learning that the patient has cancer, some families may begin to mourn him and treat him as if he were already dead. The resolution of the crisis for the patient may depend on how successfully these persons are enabled to view him as he actually may be—an individual who is coping effectively with his feeling about the diagnosis with a relatively good prognosis or at least one that suggests he can be expected to function effectively as a social being for a reasonable period of time.

The social worker must also examine his own attitudes toward the diagnosis of cancer and what he introduces into the patient's problem by virtue of the significance cancer has for him, the stress it creates in him, and how he is able to handle this. He must have conviction about the value of casework service even in situations when the goals must be limited because of the extent and nature of the patient's particular form of disease. Crisis theory, with its emphasis on the fact that help appropriately given at the right time and suitably focused may be more effective than help of a more extended nature at a time when patient or family are less emotionally accessible, strengthens the worker's conviction of the significance of his help. The fact that a goal in crisis intervention is that of encouraging and supporting the patient and/or family to develop new coping patterns should be viewed as a force in enabling them to gain strength in meeting future stressful situations by the use of the more effective adaptive and coping mechanisms they have learned.[7]

CRISIS PRONENESS

The relative strength or weakness of the patient's ego and that of the family member who plays a major role in the resolution of the problem are basic to the treatment techniques the worker selects. Often acceptance of the patient for care at a cancer research and treatment center, even though he may have been considered beyond help elsewhere, seems to be sufficiently ego supportive for him and his family to enable them to function without social work intervention. The presence of relatively weak egos in the patient and a significant other suggest the probability of other limitations and the existence of "crisis proneness" in the family as a whole that may make them more vulnerable to the situation. It also suggests the probable lack of crisis-meeting resources (economic, personality, family integration, and the like), an inability to learn from past experiences, and a tendency to view the present situation as a crisis without calling into action any problem-solving mechanism.

[7] Howard J. Parad, "Preventive Casework: Problems and Implications," in Parad, ed., *Crisis Intervention: Selected Readings* (New York: Family Service Association of America, 1965), p. 289.

6

Families who may be thought of as "crisis prone" in the crises associated with cancer follow the characteristic patterns described in the literature—they lack family integration, both material and kinship resources, meaningful relationships, and spiritual or religious faith. Prediction of a patient's capacity to adapt to his situation, even though he may be an elderly unattached man living on a marginal income and partially dependent on public assistance for support, will still be favorable when one notes a consistent prior work history, residence as a lodger in the same private household for many years, a confident but not dependent attitude toward the welfare worker, and a demonstrated capacity to involve himself in a purposeful and creative leisure-time activity. Casework with this type of individual may well be focused on enabling him to gain relief from the stress emanating from an unusually lengthy hospitalization owing to surgical complications. By helping him to verbalize his feeling about this and performing manipulative services of a minor but meaningful nature (such as facilitating repair of eyeglasses) the social worker can reassure him that he is still an individual to be valued and is worthy of attention even though his body-image may have been damaged by the fact of a colostomy or the necessity of wearing diapers because of a bladder problem related to surgery.

CRITICAL PERIODS

There appear to be certain critical periods in the course of the patient's illness when he is more apt to require social work help. If contact is initiated with the patient early in the course of his illness at a time when he may first have become aware of the nature of his illness and has not yet been able to mobilize his coping devices, the supportive role the worker uses, his assumption that the patient is able to deal with his problem—which provides the latter with a feeling of hope that also lessens his feelings of helplessness—often gives the patient enough ego support to begin to involve himself in working on his problem. The worker is thus presented with an opportunity to prevent or avert undue regression and stress at this point. This presumes that he has been able to achieve a meaningful relationship with the patient by demonstrating immediately that he is able to be helpful at that time or to be a potential source of help when needed.

This may be achieved by meeting the patient's needs during the first interview, if possible. The initial interview must be more than exploratory, for it must be combined with the therapeutic process. In the time-limited situation commonly experienced in medical settings, diagnosis and treatment go on simultaneously, usually from the beginning. The worker needs to be skillful and confident, able to select his treatment methods on the spot and on the basis of a quick and accurate diagnostic assessment. The degree of the worker's security in what he can offer has a contagious effect on the patient. The worker's obvious confidence in his own capacity to understand and to help offers a great degree of ego support to the patient. For those who are trying to cope with the new diagnosis of cancer, the knowledge of the social worker's accessibility and an awareness of his flexibility and continuing interest are important.

During the acute crisis period, underlying pre-existing problems or key emotionally relevant issues are often close to thé surface, having been reactivated by the crisis, and hence are once more accessible for treatment. The worker should therefore be able to shift back and forth between the immediate and most pressing needs as felt by the patient and the more remote problems that have been reactivated, to prevent incorporation of further maladaptive solutions by the ego, which in turn can lead to further stress and more resistive behavior when the next period of crisis arises.

In the management of the crisis situation the worker must have concrete social re-

7

sources, such as financial assistance and homemaker services, available for use if needed to back up casework techniques. Tangible evidence of other than financial support can have great significance—staying with the patient at an anxiety-producing time such as prior to surgery, accompanying the patient's spouse to a conference with the attending physician when "bad news" is anticipated, providing specific information about funeral arrangements. (Articulation of concern by the family about funeral arrangements can be considered a way of dealing with stress by taking active anticipatory steps; it is evidence of an attempt at realistic coping *provided* it occurs at the appropriate time when the physician has determined that death is imminent.)

For some patients more long-range goals are feasible because the disease has been controlled. These individuals, however, because of the surgery required to remove the tumor and prevent metastases, may need rehabilitative services ranging from speech therapy and prostheses of one type or another to vocational rehabilitation because of the physical problems associated with their former employment. If the initial casework has been adequate in enabling the patient to use his own resources for coping, once the rehabilitation program has been firmly established he can be expected to manage without assistance. Contact with the social worker is needed only if the patient encounters some entirely new problem that defies his repertoire of problem-solving devices.

USE OF TIMING

The sensitive and appropriate use of timing is one of the basic factors in crisis intervention casework. Time has always been important in the framework of social work practice in hospitals. In working with cancer patients, time has an additional dimension for the social worker and the patient and his family—especially the question of *when* for the terminally ill patient.

Catherine Gabrielson, writing of her dying child in *The Story of Gabrielle*, says:

Now we had an idea about how many [days] you had left—not the exact number but too few to speculate about. We just decided to try to live them as fully as possible with you. I thought how interested people always were in a baby's first days; last days shouldn't be any less important or interesting.[8]

This poignantly describes the stress for patient and mother and suggests the focus of the supportive relationship the social worker may offer them to enable them to prepare for the final separation, taking steps together to accelerate and deepen a close relationship. Consideration must be given to the need many patients, their families, and close friends have to conclude a meaningful relationship. This experience can be both comforting and positive if they can accomplish this. For many individuals who are not articulate or accustomed to expressing their feelings, this may be difficult or impossible, but if the caseworker has an adequate comprehension of their life-style or system of communication, he may enable them to handle this by the nonverbal means with which they are more familiar.

Some families begin to grieve during this period and, provided it is not communicated to the patient, this may help them to cope more effectively with his actual death. Parents who have lived with children's lengthy illness, characterized by brief remissions between frequent and increasingly debilitating, painful relapses, have often been observed to begin to grieve as death appears imminent. At the point the child becomes moribund, they have spontaneously expressed a wish for the end of the ordeal for the patient and themselves, feeling that "He has gone through too much," and acknowledging that the physicians and they as parents have done everything possible to help their child. They indicate a

8 Catherine Gabrielson, *The Story of Gabrielle* (Cleveland: World Publishing Co., 1956), p. 46.

8

readiness to return to meeting the needs of others within the family, especially their other children, and to get on with the process of more normal living.

CONCLUSION

As previously indicated, cancer is an emotionally charged illness. There is still a tendency on the part of a large segment of the lay public to speak of the diagnosis in hushed tones and to avoid referring to it by name. Likewise, there are still some physicians who will go to great lengths to spare the patient the knowledge that he has cancer. Many patients are willing participants in this conspiracy of silence about their illness, but are actually aware of it and realistically seek help in coping with their situation. Unconsciously they may resort to various devices to camouflage their need for help. The social worker who works with them would do well to follow Fern Lowry's observation:

> As caseworkers we really need four ears: one with which to listen to *what* is being said; one to attend to what is *not* being said; one to hear *how* it is being said; and one to heed the feelings *unexpressed*.[9]

---

[9] Fern Lowry, "The Caseworker in Short Contact Services," *Social Work*, Vol. 2, No. 1 (January 1957), p. 55.

9

This article describes the crisis intervention techniques used by the San Fernando Valley Child Guidance Clinic to help families deal with the traumatic events experienced in the 1971 earthquake in California.

Crisis intervention in an earthquake

By Herbert Blaufarb and Jules Levine

Herbert Blaufarb, Ph.D., is Chief of Treatment Services and Jules Levine, MSW, is Supervising Social Worker, San Fernando Valley Child Guidance Clinic, Van Nuys, California.

Crisis intervention is now a recognized and valuable addition to the repertoire of treatment modalities of many mental health agencies. In line with Caplan's formulation, a crisis can be characterized as an emotional reaction to an external hazardous situation, with the possibility of ensuing disorganization of behavior.[1] The individual in crisis initially calls on habitual coping mechanisms in an attempt to resolve his difficulties. If these behaviors fail, additional internal and external resources are called on. If these, too, fail, major disorganization of the personality can occur.

It is generally thought that a person in crisis is motivated to seek help and is uniquely susceptible to therapeutic intervention. Timely intervention during a crisis, therefore, can have a significant positive impact on a person's functioning.

In the San Fernando Valley Child Guidance Clinic in California parents usually present their children as manifesting a variety of symptoms, many of which are chronic in nature. Rarely do they present a clearly defined immediate problem that is readily identified as a crisis. Thus a primary focus of the initial interview is to identify the crisis, if one is present, and to distinguish between the crisis and the hazardous event that precipitated it.

A common problem encountered by most professionals who work in child guidance settings is that although children are identified as the clients, they often do not experience discomfort. Rather, it is the parents who are experiencing discomfort and seeking help because of difficulties in relating to the child or for personal problems. For these reasons, application of the crisis model in working with children presents difficulties, particularly in identifying the hazardous event that precipitated the crisis.

On February 9, 1971—the day of the earthquake—the clinic was presented with the opportunity to work with a large number of children and their families who were experiencing crisis reactions. At the time of the earthquake (6:00 A.M.) most families were in bed. They were awakened by a severe shaking of their homes; many were thrown out of their beds and were unable to stand during the thirty seconds of the initial violent shock. This prevented many parents from reaching their children until after the initial shock had subsided. When the families did reach each other, most clung together, either in a doorway or huddled in bed. Because of the damage to telephone and power lines, many homes were without electricity and the families were unable to find out if relatives and friends had been injured. Fortunately, radio and television communication remained unimpaired, and information given over the air was reassuring. Those staff members who lived in San Fernando Valley reacted quite similarly to the families seen at the clinic. This common experience undoubtedly helped the staff to empathize with the families.

On the day of the earthquake the clinic's director of clinical services went on the radio to offer help to parents and children who were frightened by the quake. In a staff conference it was decided that staff members would speak on the phone with all parents and others who called for help and that groups of such parents and children would be formed when this seemed clinically indicated. The following questions were kept in mind: When a hazard of the enormity of an earthquake occurs, what are the reactions of children and their families? Does a common hazard of such intensity lead to similar behavioral reactions in children and their families? Which crisis intervention techniques are appropriate to large numbers of people immediately following such a natural disaster?

Of the eight hundred parents who phoned, most only needed reassurance that they were reacting appropriately. The workers gave them advice about helping their children unwind by talking with them, giving them some warm milk or hot chocolate at bedtime and reading to them, using a night light, and reminding the children

they were safe and the parents would take care of them. They also urged the parents to have their children return to usual sleeping, eating, and play patterns as soon as possible. If the parents continued to express a need for further help, they were invited to come to the groups.

The choice of group counseling techniques was based on two considerations: (1) It was anticipated that many families would avail themselves of the service, many more than could be served by individual counseling and the usual intake procedures. (2) The clinic had extensive experience in developing and using crisis-oriented groups for children and their parents, e.g., the drop-in group, and more recent experience in brief family therapy.

The first group of twenty-two parents and children met the next evening. Similar groups, totaling three hundred families, met with various workers over a five-week period. The groups met for this length of time because for weeks after the initial shock, hundreds of aftershocks occurred, which re-created the horrors of the initial quake. About 85 percent of the families attended only one session. The remaining 15 percent either returned for an additional meeting or were referred for immediate short-term individual or family treatment or behavior modification groups in which desensitization techniques were used.

COMMON FEARS

Most of the children and parents reported remarkably uniform reactions. Their fears were quite similar and appropriate. However, their behaviors, which were also similar, were inappropriate. The most common problem for the children (aged 3–12) was a fear of going to sleep in their own rooms; of those who did go to their own rooms, most were unable to sleep through the night. Many were persistent in their demands to sleep with their parents and would cry, stand at the door of their parents' room, or climb into bed with their parents. This behavior was quickly reinforced by

---

[1] Gerald Caplan, *Principles of Preventive Psychiatry* (New York: Basic Books, 1964).

2

> *"The knowledge that parents could talk about their fears seemed to reassure the children. They came to understand that mobilization of physical and emotional resources in emergencies is a healthy and necessary reaction.*

the majority of mothers who took these children into their beds.

The other major problem was that many younger children (aged 3–6) were afraid to remain alone in one part of the house during the day, even though their mothers were present in another room. They were also afraid to play with other children, preferring to remain with their mothers, to whom they clung. These reactions constituted the vast bulk of complaints, although there were scattered reports of regression in toilet and eating habits. These behaviors were indicative of severe separation anxiety and represented the children's attempts to maintain contact with parents who provide safety and security.

Small children take their cues from their parents. It is difficult for frightened parents to convince frightened children that they should relax and feel safe. In addition the parents' fear interfered with parental roles. The parents expressed much uncertainty about and hesitancy in setting limits or dealing with the children's maladaptive reactions to fear, e.g., continued demands to sleep with them. It seemed that the parents were afraid to assert themselves because this would have negative and perhaps permanent psychological effects on their children. When the children continued to make demands, the parents felt angry and guilty, which confused them and made it more difficult for them to help their children. In short, most had become temporarily immobilized in their roles as parents.

INTERVENTION

In the groups intervention was geared toward both the children and their parents.

The first task was to help reduce the level of anxiety in both parents and children. The goal was to have the family reestablish itself as a unit and for the family members to reassume their usual roles as soon as possible. This involved such concrete interventions as reinstituting sleeping arrangements and helping parents reassert themselves as the guiding and steadying influences in the family.

The interventions directed toward the children basically were designed to make the children aware of their fears of losing both their parents and the stability of the home. In the group the children were encouraged to verbalize and share their thoughts and feelings about their earthquake experiences, especially their fears of losing their parents and how frightened they were when their beds shook and furniture and dishes were smashed. Even the youngest children were relieved when another child haltingly spoke of his terror. Children were pleased to discover that both their peers and their parents had similar feelings and reactions.

The knowledge that parents could talk about their fears seemed to reassure the children. They came to understand that mobilization of physical and emotional resources in emergencies is a healthy and necessary reaction. Children were able to recognize too that their regressive behavior was an attempt to get the protection and care they needed from their parents until they could feel secure enough to function as before. It was found that the quickest recoveries from the quake experience occurred in those children whose parents could understand and for the necessary brief interval accept their regressive behavior. These parents were secure enough

3

to encourage and help their children talk about their thoughts and feelings.

Intervention with parents was primarily aimed at rousing them from their uncertainty, and in some cases their immobility, and helping them reestablish normal family patterns as quickly as possible. Although the workers stressed that the parents should not take a punitive approach to their children's maladaptive behavior, parents were urged actively and firmly to encourage their children to resume their usual routines. Parents also were encouraged to involve their children as much as possible in family decision-making concerning both earthquake-related and other matters and to make more time available to them. Also it was suggested that the families discuss whatever factual information about the earthquakes was available in the media and in books.

Crisis counseling, both in the groups and in phone conversations, helped the parents resume functioning in their roles as parents. Most parents seemed to be seeking support to deal with their children as they had before the quake. The counseling also helped the parents reestablish the family as a unit and restore the usual parent-child, child-sibling, and child-peer behavioral patterns to provide the child with the security and certainty of the familiar.

Although the primary focus was on the children, the workers intervened directly with the parents when necessary. For example, one mother's complaint about her children's behavior exhibited a strong nonverbal undercurrent of overwhelming feelings of inadequacy and guilt. She blamed herself because they were still upset. The worker told her: "We're not heroes—we can only do so much." Other mothers provided feedback that said in effect: "You're all right. Like us, you've done all you could on your own and now you're here to get a little additional help." Another mother was overworked and at the point of collapse. She had a physical disability that made it impossible for her to take care of her children at that time. The workers encouraged her to arrange for the children's care while she went to her mother's home to rest. This sanction was all she needed to make these arrangements without a heavy load of guilt.

FURTHER QUESTIONS

Lack of funding prevented the clinic from doing a formal follow-up evaluation of its crisis intervention service. However, several clinical research questions, pertinent to crisis theory and crisis intervention, were raised by observing the families who had experienced the earthquake. For instance, each person maintains his emotional balance by means of specific behavioral patterns and is more prone to move into crisis if the hazardous situation corresponds to a long-standing problem area unique to him. However, if the hazard is a common one and of the enormity of an earthquake, do the reactions and coping mechanisms unique to the individuals subjected to the trauma fail, and are they replaced by reactions and coping behaviors that are similar to those of all persons who experienced the hazard? Further, how are coping mechanisms reinstituted? What course do they take as persons affected by a natural disaster go about reestablishing their homes and family units? What about the timing of the therapeutic intervention—is there an optimum point during such a crisis when the intervention will be most effective? Can crisis intervention programs be woven into the established fabric of existing emergency disaster programs?

These are only a few of the questions relevant to crisis intervention. The clinic's experience does not conclusively demonstrate that the crisis intervention model is the most appropriate and effective short-term treatment modality. However, it does show that crisis intervention is an effective technique for alleviating the negative effects of psychological trauma on those persons who have experienced a natural disaster.

4

NASW REPRINTS

NA SW

BY NAOMI GOLAN AND RUTH GRUSCHKA

Integrating the New Immigrant: A Model for Social Work Practice in Transitional States

■ *The transfer of individuals or groups to new areas or countries poses complex problems for both the immigrant and the community. The authors of this paper cast the process in the prevention-intervention framework and offer a model for activity in six key areas—income management, health, housing, education, leisure-time activities, and citizenship—by which the integration-absorption crisis can be successfully resolved.* ■

ONE OF THE inevitable side effects of political and social change is the uprooting of individuals and groups and their transfer to new communities and situations. Whether this occurs in the process of moving from one city to another, from one region to another, or from one country to another, discernible disruptions in living patterns and role functioning take place. During the mass migrations to the United States in the late nineteenth and early twentieth centuries and immediately after World War II, social workers considered the resultant problems as appropriate areas for their immediate and extensive concern. However, in recent years, although this transitional process has been examined exhaustively by sociologists, anthropologists, and

even psychologists, social workers have paid little attention to the unique adjustment problems encountered by immigrants and the communities to which they come, except for occasional anecdotal accounts.[1] Yet such situations should be of special interest to practitioners because they are frequently called on to solicit, develop, and/or administer services to newcomers.

Israelis, of course, are "old pros" on the subject of migration; their country was built on this basis, and an extensive structure of services and resettlement methods has been developed over the years. However, different phases of immigration have called for changing patterns to deal with the situation. In response to the unprecedented rise in immigration from western developed countries (including the United States and Canada) within the past few

NAOMI GOLAN, Ph.D., *is Associate Professor, School of Social Welfare, University of Wisconsin-Milwaukee. During the 1968–69 academic year, she taught at the Paul Baerwald School of Social Work, Hebrew University, Jerusalem.* RUTH GRUSCHKA, MSW, M.Sc.Hyg., *is a public health social worker at the Israel Ministry of Health and a social work consultant for the Jewish Agency, Jerusalem, Israel.*

[1] Although various authors have described the difficulties of working with immigrants, Ruth Chaskel is one of the few social workers to examine the implications of this process and the issues involved for practice since Jane Addams and Mary Simkhovitch. See "Effect of Mobility on Family Life," *Social Work*, Vol. 9, No. 4 (October 1964), pp. 83–91.

Reprinted from SOCIAL WORK, 16 (April 1971), pp. 82–87. Copyright © by the National Association of Social Workers, Inc., 1971.
CAO–013–C

years, urban absorption centers have been set up throughout the country. Newly arrived individuals or families come directly to these centers and stay for a limited period, usually up to six months. Within this benign environment in which they are protected to some degree from the pressures of Israeli daily life, immigrants can become adjusted to the country, learn the language, look for jobs and housing, settle their children in schools, and perform other transitional tasks that hopefully will lead to full-fledged integration.

As part of its services to new immigrants, the Jewish Agency stationed social workers in several absorption centers.[2] Little attention was directed, however, to the specific dimensions of their professional role in this setting and the nontraditional type of client until the issue was raised in 1968 by the Paul Baerwald School of Social Work, Hebrew University of Jerusalem, which had a fieldwork student unit in the Jerusalem center. It was decided that social work practice in this setting would be examined in order to clarify the specific methods used from the teaching aspect and to help the workers document their experiences from the practice aspect. Following is the theoretical framework developed as the first stage of the study sponsored jointly by the Baerwald school and the Jewish Agency.

THEORETICAL FRAMEWORK

Immigration consists of two complementary processes: integration into the community by the immigrating individual or family unit and absorption of newcomers by the host community.[3] The experience would certainly fall within the definition of normal transitional states, which has been a topic of interest to crisis theoreticians who postulate that during such time-limited periods of disruption, the immigrant and host community call on various coping methods to handle the disequilibrium brought on by the stressful situation.[4] It is assumed that the immigrant's decision to migrate is by definition hazardous and begins a process leading, in some cases, to a state of crisis.[5] Less explicit, but certainly as disruptive, is the dislocation experienced by the community that must open its structure, however willingly, to the newcomer. Whether the immigrant and the community are able to master the transition through customary problem-solving methods, call up new emergency measures, and emerge with adaptive patterns of functioning and new growth experiences might depend on what help was offered during this crucial time.[6]

Closely allied to the crisis formulation is the public health approach, which emphasizes that if adequate provisions can be afforded populations at risk, future dysfunction can be prevented.[7] Attention must therefore be given to the development of resources and the forestalling of potential maladaptations by anticipatory guidance through the pitfalls of the integration-absorption process. It should be noted that ultimate failure of the process is clearly visible with this clientele (i.e., the newcomer makes a poor adjustment or leaves the country or the community fails to de-

[2] The Jewish Agency, an arm of the World Zionist Organization, is an autonomous body that bears responsibility for migration of Jews to Israel. It shares this responsibility with the Israel Ministry of Absorption, but is not part of the government.

[3] Hereafter the term immigrant will be used for either the individual or family unit. The community may be the local one in which the absorption center is located, the one in which the immigrant eventually settles, or the total community of Israel.

[4] Lydia Rapoport, "Crisis-Oriented Short-Term Casework," Social Service Review, Vol. 41, No. 1 (March 1967), pp. 31–43.

[5] For an explication of the phases in a crisis situation, see Naomi Golan, "When Is a Client in Crisis?" Social Casework, Vol. 50, No. 7 (July 1969), pp. 389–394.

[6] Howard J. Parad, "Preventive Casework: Problems and Implications," in Parad, ed., Crisis Intervention: Selected Readings (New York: Family Service Association of America, 1965), pp. 293–294.

[7] Lydia Rapoport, "The Concept of Prevention in Social Work," Social Work, Vol. 6, No. 1 (January 1961), pp. 3–12.

2

velop into a receptive environment), and numerous other levels of failure or partial success may also be discerned.

Before examining the nature of current social work practice in absorption centers, the stages that clients go through during immigration must be described. The central question for study, posed in terms of Studt's formulation, was: What are the problems in social functioning, the social tasks involved in coping with these problems, and the service system needed to carry out these tasks, both from the immigrant's and the community's points of view? [8]

INTEGRATION-ABSORPTION MODEL

To answer this question, an operational model of the steps that would have to be undertaken for successful integration and absorption to occur was developed. Six potential problem areas were differentiated: income management, health, housing, education, leisure-time activities, and citizenship. Then the specific problems that might be encountered by the immigrant and/or the community within each of these areas were outlined.

The social tasks facing newcomers and communities as they attempt to solve these problems were delineated along two dimensions: "material-arrangemental" and psychosocial.[9] It was found that these tasks fall into a definite pattern. Along the material-arrangemental axis, the newcomer must do the following:

1. Explore available solutions and resources.

2. Choose an appropriate solution or resource and obtain training or eligibility to qualify for it.

3. Apply formally for the solution or resource.

---

[8] Elliot Studt, *A Conceptual Approach to Teaching Materials* (New York: Council on Social Work Education, 1965), pp. 4–18.

[9] The term "material-arrangemental" refers both to concrete assistance and environmental modification services.

4. Develop new patterns of operation, take on new roles in utilizing the solution or resource.

5. Undergo a period of supervision or apprenticeship until functioning rises to acceptable norms.

Parallel to this process, the community must:

1. Collect and make available information on possible solutions and potential resources and develop new ones if necessary.

2. Specify qualifications and eligibility and set up orientation and training programs in the use of the solution or resource.

3. Set up the apparatus and develop the procedures by which newcomers apply for the solution or resource.

4. Develop new patterns of operation that will accommodate to or include newcomers in utilizing the solution or resource.

5. Provide supervision or apprenticeship programs until the newcomers' functioning rises to acceptable norms.

These tasks, important as they are, must be accompanied by a more intangible process along the psychosocial axis. The immigrant must also do as follows:

1. Cope with the threat to past security and levels of performance.

2. Grapple with the anxieties and frustrations generated in the process of choosing the solution or resource and training for it.

3. Handle the stress generated in applying for the solution or resource.

4. Adjust to new roles and redistribute statuses within the family unit to accommodate the new patterns of operation.

5. Develop new standards of well-being and agree to diminished satisfactions until the integration process is completed.

Similarly, the community must:

1. Cope with the threat to its own past security and accustomed levels of performance.

2. Grapple with the anxieties and frustrations of both newcomers and old-timers when the solution or resource is offered and during the training period.

Task for Immigrant	Task for Community
1. Explore available income sources: work, pension, social security, transfer payments, stipends, special grants, loans, private resources (savings, relatives, and so on); investigate shopping facilities, banking arrangements, investment opportunities, alternate ways of handling money.	1. Compile and make available a directory of job opportunities, data on social security, welfare payments, special benefits, union qualifications, income tax waivers, and so forth; canvass community for potential positions for hard-to-place persons; set up shopping and savings arrangements familiar to and convenient for newcomers.
2. Select job opportunity in which interested; learn qualifications, obtain proper preparation; check eligibility, local regulations regarding money transfers, banking arrangements, credit union, check-cashing, and so forth.	2. Specify qualifications for various jobs and eligibility regulations; set up orientation and training programs for jobs, purchasing, investment, tax information, and money management; train community residents in spending and purchasing habits of the newcomers.
3. Apply for job, social security, stipend, and so forth; arrange for credit, bank accounts, buying of food, clothing, household needs; join union, professional organizations.	3. Accept job applications and bring together employers and potential employees; process applications for credit, banking services, and currency tranfers; induct applicants into unions and professional groups.
4. Begin to develop new working skills and work patterns; start adjusting to new conditions, shopping hours, purchasing habits, spending and saving patterns; learn new ways to keep house, cook, use domestic help, and so forth.	4. Adjust working arrangements to make use of newcomers' skills and to accommodate new working styles; make accommodations regarding newcomers' shopping hours, purchasing habits, salaries, child care needs; develop new opportunities for investments; open new facilities for buying and spending.
5. Arrange for and accept supervision; enter into apprenticeship programs until productivity and income rises to acceptable norms; solicit periodic help from neighbors and friends in adapting to local ways of buying and spending, seasonal needs, and the like.	5. Arrange for and set up supervisory or apprenticeship programs until newcomers' productivity and income rise to acceptable norms; set up periodic demonstration projects and follow-up programs on buying and spending.

3. Tolerate the stress generated by conflicting demands, new needs, and different modes of behavior when newcomers apply for the solution or resource.

4. Redefine old roles and redistribute statuses within the community to include newcomers in patterns of operation and hierarchical structures.

5. Develop new standards of acceptable performance and accept diminished returns until the absorption process is completed.

The appropriate service systems that might be expected to carry out the two sets of tasks most appropriately and economically were defined. This was seen as the operational aspect of the study; it would vary with each situation and ideally would result in a multiple prescription for action to be carried out in the absorption center—in some cases by the immigrant himself, in others by the community (as represented by a specific facility or community care-giver), and in still others, jointly or in various combinations.

SOCIAL WORKER'S ROLE

The use of this model would result in the social worker's role primarily becoming that of enabler or catalyst. He would work along with the immigrant and community to survey the situation in terms of potential problems, indicate the social tasks to be performed, and investigate the services available if the situation called for it. Then he

TABLE 2. PSYCHOSOCIAL TASKS IN INTEGRATION-ABSORPTION PROCESS: INCOME MANAGEMENT

Task for Immigrant	Task for Community
1. Cope with threat to past job security, levels of work performance, earnings, income limitations, and accustomed ways of handling money.	1. Cope with threat to prestige and job security of present job incumbents, previous levels of work performance, salary scales, customary ways of handling money, and sources of income.
2. Grapple with anxieties and frustrations in transitional state while investigating job opportunities and struggling with unfamiliar currency, modes of shopping, bill payments, check-writing, and so forth.	2. Grapple with anxieties and frustrations of potential employers, unions, and the like in arranging for training programs; explain need for unfamiliar regulations and procedures.
3. Handle feelings of stress and insecurity generated by applying for job, social security, admission to professional group, and the like; deal with worries regarding currency arrangements, credit loans, and financial security.	3. Tolerate the stress and negative attitudes of employers and job incumbents; accept stress reactions of newcomers in applying for jobs, money transfers, setting up currency arrangements, and so forth.
4. Adjust to new work roles (e.g., from self-employed to worker); redistribute family statuses (from housewife to breadwinner, husband to student); take on new family roles for shopping, child care, and so on to accommodate to new conditions.	4. Redefine old roles in employer-employee relations, redistribute statuses (from worker-oriented to middle-class society) to accommodate to new values in income management, permit newcomers to participate and rise in economic hierarchy.
5. Develop new standards of "good" job, "necessary" living arrangements, and acceptable range of buying and spending until integration process is completed.	5. Develop new standards of "acceptable" job performance, reduce pressures and demands on newcomer, live with reduced expectations and increased anxiety engendered by new competitors until absorption process is completed.

would inform the two client systems of the available options, help them weigh the consequences of alternative solutions or resources, and help them decide on an eventual course of action. In addition, he might take on such ancillary practitioner role functions as providing support, giving advice, permitting ventilation of feelings, warning of possible dangers, and rehearsing for reality.

When appropriate services were not available, the social worker might shift to the advocate or innovator role. It would then be his task to push for the development of new services, restructuring of existing ones, and overcoming the lethargy and resistance to change that are an inevitable part of service systems. On occasion, he might assume the role of mediator or collective bargainer to bring client groups and bureaucratic structures together.[10]

[10] *See* Harry Specht, "Casework Practice and Social Policy Formulation," *Social Work*, Vol. 13, No. 1 (January 1968), pp. 42–52.

Because explication of the social tasks in the integration-absorption process is the heart of this model, the application of the model to one of the six problem areas will be illustrated in order to indicate how quickly abstract theory can be translated into concrete reality situations.

Income management refers to all those activities concerned with obtaining and spending an income. It involves all aspects of looking for and obtaining jobs, salary negotiations, money transfers, currency exchange, shopping for food and other items, dealing with financial institutions, and so on. A detailed illustration of the material-arrangemental and psychosocial tasks in the income management area for both immigrant and community are shown in Tables 1 and 2.

Health alludes to existing medical and

5

paramedical needs such as services of a physician, dentist, hospital, diagnostic or laboratory technician, public health nurse, physiotherapist, and nursing home; prepaid hospitalization and medical care insurance plans; and the like. It also refers to potential health hazards that arise from new climatic conditions or local patterns of nutrition and sanitation.

Housing deals both with accommodations desired and arrangements available in terms of size of units; floor plans and internal arrangements; rental or purchase of single or multiple dwellings; costs; financing arrangements; and accessibility to schools, jobs, shopping facilities, transportation, public utilities, recreational facilities, and so forth.

Education refers primarily to the formal education facilities for primary, secondary, and higher education, as well as special education needs of individual members of a family unit (e.g., school for the deaf or music lessons) or a specific age group (e.g., the difficulties incurred by adolescents studying in a foreign language in an unfamiliar cultural setting with undefined expectations for educational achievement). Kindergartens and preschool programs also are covered. Religious or agricultural orientation could well be the determining factors in this area.

Leisure-time activities is a blanket term for the cultural, social, recreational, and religious needs and interests of the immigrant and for the facilities of the community. These activities may range from movies or concerts to sports or Sabbath services. The term also refers to the informal arrangements through which newcomers often become socialized into a community (e.g., kaffeeklatsches, backyard barbecues, and jam sessions).

Citizenship alludes to the rights and obligations that the newcomer faces in his to-be-adopted country (e.g., voting, military service, taxes, political affiliation, and identification with special interest pressure groups). These rights and obligations are often considered only hazily before immigration, but they soon assume concrete reality in a country like Israel, with its demands for active citizen involvement and participation.

This model postulates that the same five-step process of exploration, choice-making, application, role-taking, and apprenticeship must be carried out in each of the six problem areas by both immigrant and community along both the material-arrangemental and psychosocial axes for the integration-absorption process to be completed.

How much of the integration-absorption process is the concern of the social worker stationed in the absorption center? Obviously, with aggressive, competent, knowledgeable immigrants, the worker can be nominally involved or even remain on the sidelines. At the other extreme, with immobilized, frightened, overwhelmed persons, he may intervene actively on all levels throughout the period that the newcomer remains in the center and even beyond. Most situations probably will fall somewhere in between. It was hypothesized in this study that by anticipating potential trouble and alerting both the immigrant and the community to what might be in store for them, disequilibrium could be held to a minimum and the integration-absorption process carried out successfully.

Crisis theoreticians have noted that a transitional state can be a period of opportunity as well as danger. Thus the social worker in the absorption center, in helping both newcomer and community to grapple with the complexities of the integration-absorption process, may have the pivotal role in determining the success of the outcome.

6